Using the Internet to Investigate Business

Ken Kaser

J. WESTON

WALCH

PUBLISHER

Portland, Maine

User's Guide
to
Walch Reproducible Books

As part of our general effort to provide educational materials that are as practical and economical as possible, we have designated this publication a "reproducible book." The designation means that purchase of the book includes purchase of the right to limited reproduction of all pages on which this symbol appears:

Here is the basic Walch policy: We grant to individual purchasers of this book the right to make sufficient copies of reproducible pages for use by all students of a single teacher. This permission is limited to a single teacher, and does not apply to entire schools or school systems, so institutions purchasing the book should pass the permission on to a single teacher. Copying of the book or its parts for resale is prohibited.

Any questions regarding this policy or requests to purchase further reproduction rights should be addressed to:

Permissions Editor
J. Weston Walch, Publisher
321 Valley Street • P. O. Box 658
Portland, Maine 04104-0658

1   2   3   4   5   6   7   8   9   10
ISBN 0-8251-4267-9

Contents

About the Author

Ken Kaser is an award-winning educator who has taught business education in Nebraska and marketing education in Texas for more than 20 years. He is the marketing coordinator at Clements High School in Sugar Land, Texas. Mr. Kaser has served as president of the Nebraska State Business Education Association (NSBEA) and the Mountain-Plains Business Education Association (M-PBEA). He has received the Outstanding Secondary Business Teacher of the Year Award from the National Business Education Association, M-PBEA, NSBEA, and Texas Business Education Association. Ken has written high school distance learning courses for Nebraska and Texas, and business and marketing curricula for Texas. Ken is also the author of *61 Cooperative Learning Activities for Business Classes* and *10-Minute Critical Thinking Activities for the World of Work*, all published by J. Weston Walch. *Sports and Entertainment Marketing* (South-Western Publishing) was co-authored by Ken Kaser.

To the Teacher

The Internet has had a huge effect on the way people do business. It has created a new way for companies to contact potential customers—some companies have been created to have only a Web presence, and many "brick-and-mortar" stores have been able to increase their customer base after setting up a web site to sell their products.

The Internet is also an extraordinary source of information. Businesses and individuals can use the Internet to find information on an astonishing array of topics, much more quickly than through the use of a library or other paper resources.

To be effective employees in this electronic world, students must learn to use the Internet. *Using the Internet to Investigate Business* will help them master the medium. Each activity guides students step-by-step through an important aspect of business Internet use, from choosing a potential career to researching countries for international trade. As students gather information, they also learn how to synthesize information from various sources, as well as how to analyze web sites for validity. Throughout the activities, students remain actively engaged, solving meaningful problems with real-world applications.

Acceptable Use Policies

Most districts and schools have "acceptable use" policies for Internet use. Check your school or district's policy prior to allowing students access to the Internet. All students should be aware of the policy before using any of these activities, and should know the penalty for policy infringements.

How to Use the Lessons and Activities

The lessons and student activities in this book are straightforward and easy to use. Each lesson addresses one important element of the business curriculum. To get the most out of each lesson, take a moment to read through the suggestions that follow.

Using the Internet

Using these lessons requires a basic understanding of how to use the Internet. At a minimum, you should be able to enter a web site address, also referred to as a Universal Resource Locator (URL), and "bookmark," or save the address of, a web page for future use. If you've never been on-line or can't do either of these tasks, don't panic. Most of the students in your class will be able to show you how to do them in less than five minutes. Learning to use the Internet takes some time but it is well worth the effort.

Verifying Web Pages

Although the web pages used in the activities were verified prior to publication, many web sites or portions thereof come and go without explanation or warning. It's important to verify the selected web pages before using the lesson. This isn't difficult and only takes a couple of minutes. To verify a web site, enter the URL in the address window of your browser, then press "enter." If the URL is functioning, you will be taken to the web page. If this does not work, or you get an error message, check that you entered the address correctly. It's easy to make a mistake entering an address, and the Internet is exacting; the address must be typed in exactly as it appears in the text. (It can be helpful to think of web addresses as more like phone numbers than mailing addresses. If you write the wrong street number on a letter, the letter may still reach the correct destination, but if you enter the wrong digit on a phone number, you don't reach the person you wanted.) If you have entered the address correctly and the site still will not come up, wait a short while and try again. Sometimes the computers that host web sites become inaccessible for short periods of time.

If you still can't access the web site after waiting and retrying the URL, the site may no longer be working. In that case, identify an alternate site to use for the activity. Details on how to do this are included in the section on "Conducting Searches" below.

If you do need to use an alternate web site for an activity, check to see if the specific directions to students need to be altered. Often, several different web sites will provide essentially the same information, but the syntax of the site will vary slightly. Depending on the extent of the changes, you may want to write them on the student handout before reproducing it, or you may just want to explain the changes orally to the class.

Computer Access

Having limited access to computers does not preclude using these activities. Most of the lessons are designed so that computer time is kept to a minimum. For example, students might visit a web page for a couple of minutes to gather information, which they then synthesize or analyze off-line. If you have limited access to computers, have students rotate their use. If your classroom only has one computer with Internet access, make one or two students responsible for gathering the lesson data and sharing the information with the class, or rotate groups of students as appropriate.

Many schools are set up with computers in a central location, such as in a computer lab or school library. If this is the case, complete the sections of the activity that can be done in class without Internet access, then use your lab time to gather the necessary information to continue or complete the lesson. Another option is to have students look up some of the information at home or in a public library with Internet access.

Activity Structure

Each activity includes a teacher guide section and reproducible student pages. The teacher guide for each activity presents an overview of the activity, a brief listing of some of the most important business topics covered, learning objectives, web sites, web search terms, suggestions for presenting the activity, and approaches to evaluation. When appropriate, selected or suggested answers are included. Many activities also offer suggestions for extensions.

Business Topics Covered

The lessons in this book are organized into topic areas. Each lesson can be used to support or extend a business topic that you are working on in class or to introduce a new one. The general business content areas that each activity covers are shown in the National Business Education Association Standards Correlation on page *viii*.

Suggestions

The lesson plans include suggestions on how to present the material, including approaches to arranging students for the activities. Some of the lessons are best for individual student work, others are more appropriate for students working in pairs, and some lessons work best for groups of students. The final decision on how to organize your students is, of course, up to you.

In some activities, suggestions also address ways to introduce the activity, or aspects of the activity that some students may find challenging. As always, you are the best judge of your students. Adopt these suggestions, adapt them, or develop your own approach. The key is to find the best way to use the activities in your class, with your students.

Evaluation and Assessment

Because the activities are designed to be open-ended, evaluation may be a challenge at first. To help you assess student responses, a generic scoring rubric is included (see appendix) for use as a guide when evaluating student work. You may wish to tailor the scoring rubric to fit the individual activities, or you may choose to develop your own means of assessment. Where appropriate, selected answers are provided on the teacher page for that activity.

Time Considerations

Since students' ability levels and schools' schedules vary greatly, time suggestions for the lessons are not given. Review the activities and decide how many class periods would be appropriate to spend on each particular lesson. Many activities can be shortened or extended by omitting parts of the activity, or adding the extension activities suggested on the teacher page.

Web Browser Software

The lessons in this book are not dependent on using any particular web browser software, e.g., Netscape® or Internet Explorer®; however, having the most current version of your browser will facilitate optimal presentation and full use of each activity's options.

Conducting Searches

Lesson-specific web sites are provided for each activity; as mentioned earlier, you should make it a practice to verify those web sites prior to using each lesson. If you find that a referenced web site is no longer valid, you will need to locate a substitute site. To simplify this, we have included appropriate search terms for each activity. Using your favorite search engine, enter the specified keywords. The search results are returned in the order of relevance according to how they match up with your keywords. Read the descriptions for the top ten or so web sites and decide if any of them have what you are searching for. If you think a web site contains the information you need, visit (by clicking on the highlighted text) and evaluate the contents. Be sure to bookmark the sites that you will want to use. Sometimes searching for that perfect web site takes a little work, but if you're persistent and thorough, you will eventually find what you're looking for.

Stay in Touch

If you find alternate web sites that will work with the lessons let us know by sending e-mail to us at: editorial@mail.walch.com.

Correlation to NBEA Standards for Business Education

Activity	Business Content Area	Standard
1. Choosing a Career	Career Development	I—Self Awareness II—Career Research IV—Career Strategy
	Information Systems	V—Communications Systems and Networking
	Economics and Personal Finance	XV—Making Career Choices
2. Preparing a Résumé	Career Development	I—Self Awareness V—School-to-Work Transition
	Communications	IV—Employment Communications
3. Successful Interviews	Career Development	V—School-to-Work Transition
	Communications	II—Social Communications IV—Employment Communications
4. The Magic of Compound Interest	Economics and Personal Finance	X—The Role of Consumers
	Computation	II—Number Relationships and Operations VI—Problem-Solving Applications
5. Comparison Shopping	Economics and Personal Finance	II—Personal Decision Making X—The Role of Consumers
6. Researching Corporate Giants	Career Development	II—Career Research
	Communications	I—Foundations of Communications III—Technological Communications
7. Global Culture and Business	International Business	I—Awareness II—International Business Communications III—Environment IV—Ethics V—Finance VIII—Import/Export and Balance of Trade
	Economics and Personal Finance	XIV—International Economic Concepts
	Entrepreneurship	VII—Global Markets
8. Global Business Ethics	International Business	IV—Ethics VII—International Marketing
	Business Law	I—Basics of the Law
	Entrepreneurship	VIII—Legal
9. Business Travel	International Business	V—Finance
	Computation	IV—Measurements
10. News and Its Impact on Business	Interrelationship of Business Functions	
11. Learning About Small Business/ Entrepreneurship	Business Law	IV—Business Organizations
	Entrepreneurship Education	I—Characteristics III—Economics VI—Management
12. Insurance and Taxes for Business	Accounting	IV—Special Applications
	Business Law	VI—Commercial Paper, Insurance, Secured Transactions, Bankruptcy
	Entrepreneurship Education	VII—Legal

Choosing a Career

Overview:

Many high school students have already developed a focused career plan, but some still don't know what they want to do after graduation. This activity shows students how to use the Internet in order to assess their own career interests and aptitudes and to choose possible career directions. They then do research to find out more about three possible careers, and see how well their high school coursework is preparing them for these careers.

Business Topics:

Career development, self-assessment, career research, career planning

Learning Objectives:

- Assess interests and aptitudes
- Identify several possible careers
- Research to learn skills, training requirements, work environment, etc. for different careers
- Correlate required skills and high school coursework

Web Sites:

Indiana Commission for Higher Education
http://icpac.indiana.edu/infoseries/is-50pl.htm

INTEC College Career Match
http://www.intec.edu.za/career/career.htm

The Career Key
http://www.ncsu.edu/careerkey/you/

Occupational Outlook Handbook
http://stats.bls.gov/ocohome.htm

California Job Star
http://jobstar.org/tools/career/spec-car.htm

Keywords for Web Searches:

- aptitude assessment
- career development
- career research

Suggestions:

1. This activity is divided into three parts. In Part I, students perform an aptitude assessment to identify some possible future careers; in Part II, they research three careers; and in Part III, they correlate the skills needed for these careers with their high school coursework. Depending on scheduling, you may have students complete all three parts in one class session, do one part each day for three class sessions, or do some or all of the parts at home.

2. The aptitude assessment section of this activity should be done by students working individually. However, Part III of the activity, correlating required skills and high school coursework, may be done in small groups, as students may find that brainstorming with others helps them identify correlations between what they are studying and the skills they need to develop.

3. You may want to introduce this activity by asking students to brainstorm possible careers, which you can list on the board or on an overhead. Encourage students to list less common jobs as well as the "biggies" (doctor, lawyer, actor, rap artist). You might include some of the following: cartographer; phlebotomist; window dresser; volcanologist; underwriter; millwright; glazier. When you have a reasonably extensive list, read off the jobs one by one, asking students if they personally know anyone who has each job listed. Ask students how they would go about learning more about any of these jobs. Then

distribute the student handouts, and have them complete the activity.

4. Some of the aptitude assessment sites may require students to register with the site first. Make sure students are aware of school or class policy regarding use of real names and e-mail addresses in such cases.

Evaluation:

Evaluate Part I and Part II for completeness of information gathered. Evaluate Part III for reasonableness of the correlations between skills and coursework, and for completeness of the career plan in Wrapping It Up.

Extensions:

- Students complete aptitude assessments on at least three different web sites, listing all the career choices suggested by each assessment. They then develop a chart comparing and contrasting the results from all three sites, and answer the following questions:

1. Which careers were suggested by all three sites?

2. Which were suggested by two sites?

3. Which were suggested by only one site?

4. Is there a correlation between your own assessment of your strengths and interests and the careers that appear on all three lists?

5. What might account for differences between lists?

- Students identify a specific company where people with the career they are interested in work. Using the Internet, students research the company to determine whether or not they would want to work there.

- Students identify the postsecondary educational requirements for their desired career, then research institutions offering that training to see whether they are on track for completing the requirements for entry to that course of training.

Name _____ Date _____

Choosing a Career

There are thousands of possible careers to choose from. Some are well known—doctor, teacher, police officer. Some are a little more obscure—actuary, gaffer, bailiff. How do you choose the career that's right for you? And once you've chosen a career, how do you get the training and skills you'll need for that kind of work?

Part I: Assess Yourself

A good way to get started is to do a job aptitude assessment. Go to one of the web sites listed below. Take the aptitude or interest assessment presented on the site.

Indiana Commission for Higher Education
http://icpac.indiana.edu/infoseries/is-50pl.htm

INTEC College Career Match
http://www.intec.edu.za/career/career.htm

The Career Key
http://www.ncsu.edu/careerkey/you/

Write the name of the web site you chose here: _____

Based on the assessment you did, choose three careers that might fit your interests and aptitudes. Write them here.

Possible Careers		
Career 1	Career 2	Career 3

(continued)

Using the Internet to Investigate Business

Choosing a Career *(continued)*

Part II: Research Careers

How much do you already know about these careers? What kind of work does a person in this career do? What are the work hours? Is any special training required? Is the work highly paid?

In the first row of the chart below, list the three careers you chose in Part I. Then fill in the other rows with what you think each career involves. For example, if one of your career choices was "pediatrician," your answers might be: Row 2—diagnosing and treating sick children; Row 3—hospital/medical office; Row 4—varies, can involve shiftwork, often requires 60+ hours per week; Row 5—4 years of undergraduate school, 4 years of medical school, 3 years internship and residency; and Row 6—high.

Career			
Work involves			
Work setting			
Hours/Schedule			
Training/Education			
Pay (high, medium, low)			

Now, find out how accurate your knowledge about these careers really is. Go to the following web sites to research your careers. Use the information you find to fill in the information in the chart on page 5.

Occupational Outlook Handbook
http://stats.bls.gov/ocohome.htm

California Job Star
http://jobstar.org/tools/career/spec-car.htm

(continued)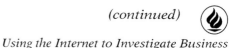

Name _____ Date _____

Choosing a Career *(continued)*

	Career 1: _____	Career 2: _____	Career 3: _____
Training			
Skills Required			
Work Setting			
Work Hours			
Job Outlook			
Job Location			
Wage Range			
Number of People in Profession			
Related Occupations			
Other			

Think About It

1. Are the three careers you chose similar to each other, or are they very different? _____

   _____

2. Does one have a much better—or much worse—job outlook than the others? _____

   _____

3. Do all three call for similar training, or do they need different skills? _____

   _____

4. Based on the information you have found out about all three careers, which one are

   you most interested in now? _____

(continued)

Choosing a Career *(continued)*

Part III: Correlate Your Career and Your Classes

In order to have the career you want, you need to start preparing now. Look carefully at the skills required for the career you are most interested in. Choose the four most important skills for that career, and list them in the first column of the chart below. In the second column, list any classes you have already taken that develop each skill you listed. For example, if one of the skills needed for your chosen career is "excellent written communication skills," you would list that in Column 1. In Column 2 you might list "English composition class." In Column 3, list any courses you are currently taking that help develop these key skills. Finally, in Column 4, list any courses you could take in the future that would help develop these skills.

Key Skill	Courses I Have Taken	Courses I Am Taking Now	Future Courses

Wrapping It Up

1. Based on the skills required for the career you chose, write a paragraph describing how you plan to get the skills and training required for the job.

_____

_____

_____

_____

_____

_____

_____

_____

Preparing a Résumé

Overview:

A well-developed résumé is a key step in the job-search process. In this activity, students begin by determining what elements are generally considered essential parts of a résumé. Next, they assemble the information they'll need to complete these elements. Finally, students enter their information in an on-line résumé generator and print out the result.

Business Topics:

Career development, school-to-work transition, résumé preparation

Learning Objectives:

- Identify essentials of a résumé
- Gather the information needed for résumé development
- Use a web site to generate a résumé
- Identify possible résumé blunders

Web Sites:

Résumé essentials

 JobWeb
http://www.jobweb.com/catapult/Guenov/how_to.html

University of Pittsburgh Placement and Career Services
http://www.placement.pitt.edu/html/resume.html

University of Maine Career Center
http://cardinal.umeais.maine.edu/~career/res.html#what

Purdue University's Online Writing Lab
http://owl.english.purdue.edu/workshops/hypertext/ResumeW/index.html

George Mason University Career Services
http://www.gmu.edu/departments/cdc/job_hunt/resume.htm

Résumé format

University of Wisconsin at Milwaukee Career Development Center
http://www.uwm.edu/Dept/CDC/resume-examples.htm

University of Vermont Career Services
http://career.uvm.edu/students/resume/format.html#Chronological

Compu-Clinic
http://www.compu-clinic.com/CLINIC/RESUME/FORMAT.HTM

Northern Illinois University Career Center
http://niu.placementmanual.com/resume/resume-03.html

Sample résumés

Quintessential Careers
http://www.quintcareers.com/resume_samples.html

Action words

The Monster Board
http://content.monster.com/resume/resources/phrases_verbs

University of Maine Career Center
http://www.ume.maine.edu/~career/action.html

Résumé generators

10 Minute Resume
http://www.10minuteresume.com

Seeking Success
http://www.seekingsuccess.com/resgen.php3

Job Smart
http://qctimes.webpoint.com/job/crg.htm

Virtualville Employment Agency
http://www.virtualville.com/employment_
agency/resume_form.html

Résumé blunders

The Monster Board
http://content.monster.com/resume/
resources/resumeblunders/

The Black Collegian Online
http://www.black-collegian.com/career/
archives/resume1299.shtml

Yahoo Career Center
http://careers.yahoo.com/employment/wsj/
story.html?s=n/emp/wsj/resumes/2.html

Headhunter.net
http://www.headhunter.net/JobSeeker/
CareerBYTES/hints0199.htm

CareerWeb
http://www.careerweb.com/rescen/
car_advice/resume/25_awful_res.html

Keywords for Web Searches:

- résumé tips
- résumé generator
- résumé resources

Suggestions:

1. Students may work individually or in small groups to complete Part I and Part II of this activity. Part III and Part IV should be completed by students working individually.

2. When students have completed Part I of the activity, you may want to have them share their findings with the class. Different web sites (like different print publications) list different elements as essential. Initiate a discussion by asking students why they think this might be. Are some elements important at one stage of a person's career, but less important at a later stage? Can the class come to a consensus as to the résumé elements that are most important for someone starting a career immediately after high school or college?

3. Some students may find Part III challenging, particularly when it comes to writing about work experience. Before students begin this

part of the activity, you might want to demonstrate this process. Have one or two students describe their experience on one job, using full sentences. Then, as a class, generate action verbs that could be used for each element of the job. Model turning sentences into phrases; emphasize that the pronoun "I" should be avoided. Then, as students work individually to complete this section, circulate to check on students' progress. If some students are still writing full sentences, or are not using action verbs, guide them through the process.

Evaluation:

Most answers in this activity will vary, depending on the sites students visit and their own information. Evaluate for the completeness of the charts and the finished résumé.

Suggested Answers:

Here are the elements that should appear in the sections requiring students to synthesize information from the web sites they visit.

Key elements of a résumé

Contact Information; Objective; Education; Experience; Other (Honors, Activities, Awards, etc.); References

Most common résumé formats

Chronological (sometimes called reverse chronological); Functional; Combination résumé

Top ten things not to do on a résumé

Student lists will vary, but should include ten items similar to the following:

Typos or grammatical errors

Focus on job duties, without showing you made a difference to the company

Focus on your needs, not the company's

Vague statement of job objective

Wrong length—either too short or too long

Use personal pronouns ("I" and "me") and articles ("an" and "the")

Include personal or irrelevant information

Use the wrong résumé format

Sloppy presentation—dirty, wrinkled,
handwritten, etc.

Too many big words

Unprofessionalism

Use lots of different fonts in order to catch the
reader's attention

Print the résumé on colored paper, or on paper
of an unusual size

Include salary requirements

Extensions:

- While print résumés are still an important
job-search tool, many companies are now

using scannable résumés. In these résumés,
two things are essential: avoiding the use of
typographical frills like different fonts and
italics, which a scanner might misread; and
including keywords that a computer might
be programmed to check for. Have students
research the essentials of a scannable
résumé, then develop a list of keywords
to use in their own résumés.

- Have students find a job that interests
them, either on-line or in a print publication, then prepare a cover letter for that
job and a résumé tailored for the specific
position.

Name _____ Date _____

Preparing a Résumé

Looking for a job—and getting the job you want—is quite a process. It starts with identifying the career you want, and getting the skills and training needed for that career. It ends when you and an employer agree on your work, salary, and benefits. But there are a lot of steps between those two points.

Part I: Essential Elements of a Résumé

One important step in the process is developing a **résumé**. This is a document—either paper or electronic—that tells potential employers about you. There are many different ways to prepare a résumé. Still, most employers expect to see certain things on a résumé, no matter what format you use. How much do you already know about résumé preparation? On the lines below, list five important elements you should include on a résumé.

Key Elements of a Résumé

1. _____

2. _____

3. _____

4. _____

5. _____

Now, find out what some on-line career information sites have to say about résumés. Go to at least three of the web sites listed below. Read what they have to say about the key elements of a résumé. In the chart below, give the URLs of the sites you visited. Then list the elements each site identified as the most important.

JobWeb
http://www.jobweb.com/catapult/Guenov/how_to.html

University of Pittsburgh Placement and Career Services
http://www.placement.pitt.edu/html/resume.html

University of Maine Career Center
http://cardinal.umeais.maine.edu/~career/res.html#what

Purdue University's Online Writing Lab
http://owl.english.purdue.edu/workshops/hypertext/ResumeW/index.html

George Mason University Career Services
http://www.gmu.edu/departments/cdc/job_hunt/resume.htm

(continued)

         Using the Internet to Investigate Business

Preparing a Résumé *(continued)*

Key Elements of a Résumé
Site 1:_____ _____ _____
Site 2:_____ _____ _____
Site 3:_____ _____ _____

Part II: Choose a Résumé Format

There is no one "right" way to create a résumé; your résumé should be as individual as you are yourself. However, there are some standard ways to present the information in a résumé. Depending on your background and experience, and on the job you're applying for, one format may be better than another for your résumé. Go to two of these web sites and read the descriptions of résumé formats.

University of Wisconsin at Milwaukee Career Development Center
http://www.uwm.edu/Dept/CDC/resume-examples.htm

University of Vermont Career Services
http://career.uvm.edu/students/resume/format.html#Chronological

Compu-Clinic
http://www.compu-clinic.com/CLINIC/RESUME/FORMAT.HTM

Northern Illinois University Career Center
http://niu.placementmanual.com/resume/resume-03.html

Write the names of the most common formats here.

1. _____

2. _____

3. _____

(continued)

Name _____ Date _____

Preparing a Résumé *(continued)*

Now, look at the way other people have put their résumés together. Go to this web site, and look at at least four of the sample résumés listed.

Quintessential Careers
http://www.quintcareers.com/resume_samples.html

In the first column of the chart below, write the name on each résumé you looked at. In the second column, write the format you think that résumé writer used. In the third column, indicate whether or not this format would be appropriate for your résumé.

	Name	**Format**	**Appropriate/Not Appropriate**
Résumé 1			
Résumé 2			
Résumé 3			
Résumé 4			

Part III: Gather Information

Before you can actually write your résumé, you need to gather all the information to complete the key elements of a résumé. Use the spaces on these pages to organize your information. As you complete this section, remember the way the résumés you looked at in Part II were written. While you don't want to copy them, you may want to imitate their style and approach.

Identifying Information

Name: _____
Address: _____
Telephone number (including area code): _____
E-mail address: _____
Web address, if you have one: _____

Job Objective

A position in which _____
_____
_____

(continued)

Preparing a Résumé *(continued)*

Work Experience

When you are describing your work experience, there are two important things to keep in mind. First, don't write in complete sentences; use short phrases. And second, use "action" verbs to describe what you did. For example, instead of saying "I was responsible for the preparation and filing of minutes of meetings," say, "Prepared and filed minutes of meetings." Look at these web sites for lists of action verbs to use in describing your work.

> The Monster Board
> http://content.monster.com/resume/resources/phrases_verbs

> University of Maine Career Center
> http://www.ume.maine.edu/~career/action.html

Most recent job

Employer name: _____

Employer address: _____

Dates of employment: from _____ to _____

Job title: _____

Duties/Responsibilities: _____

_____

_____

_____

Previous job

Employer name: _____

Employer address: _____

Dates of employment: from _____ to _____

Job title: _____

Duties/Responsibilities: _____

_____

_____

_____

If you have had more than two jobs, use the back of this sheet to list them. Be sure to include all the required information for each job.

(continued)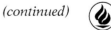

Preparing a Résumé *(continued)*

Education

School name: _____
City, state: _____
Year of graduation: _____
Diploma/degree/certificate: _____
Major programs studied: _____
Academic achievements, honors, awards: _____
Extracurricular activities: _____

Other

This is a place to list information that just doesn't fit in any of the other sections, but that it might be helpful for an employer to know. For example, if you speak more than one language fluently, or have extensive computer programming skills, put that information here. But remember, **be specific**. For example, don't just say "Bilingual;" say, "Fluent in English and Mandarin."

(continued)

Preparing a Résumé *(continued)*

Part IV: Create Your Résumé

Now that you have organized the information you'll need for a résumé, you're ready to put it all together.

Go to one of the web sites listed below. Follow the directions to create your own résumé. When the résumé is finished, print it out.

10 Minute Resume
http://www.10minuteresume.com

Seeking Success
http://www.seekingsuccess.com/resgen.php3

Job Smart
http://qctimes.webpoint.com/job/crg.htm

Virtualville Employment Agency
http://www.virtualville.com/employment_agency/resume_form.html

Résumé Blunders

Your résumé is an important tool for finding a job. It is the first impression a potential employer has of you. So you need to be sure your résumé gives the impression you want it to give. Some people forget this important fact. They make mistakes in résumé preparation that cost them the chance of an interview. Go to three of these web sites to see the kinds of mistakes people make. Then, on the lines below, make a Top Ten list of "Things Not to Do on a Résumé."

The Monster Board
http://content.monster.com/resume/resources/resumeblunders/

The Black Collegian Online
http://www.black-collegian.com/career/archives/resume1299.shtml

Yahoo Career Center
http://careers.yahoo.com/employment/wsj/story.html?s=n/emp/wsj/resumes/2.html

Headhunter.net
http://www.headhunter.net/JobSeeker/CareerBYTES/hints0199.htm

CareerWeb
http://www.careerweb.com/rescen/car_advice/resume/25_awful_res.html

(continued)

Preparing a Résumé *(continued)*

Top Ten Things Not to Do on a Résumé

1. _____

2. _____

3. _____

4. _____

5. _____

6. _____

7. _____

8. _____

9. _____

10. _____

Successful Interviews

Overview:

This activity gives students an opportunity to learn about effective interviewing techniques. After visiting several web sites, students compile a list of interview tips and blunders. They then research to find some common interview questions, and prepare their own answers to these questions. Finally, they compile all the information into a brochure designed to help interviewees succeed.

Business Topics:

Career development, critical thinking, interview preparation

Learning Objectives:

- Identify and synthesize best practices for interview preparation
- Identify and analyze interview blunders
- Determine commonly asked interview questions, and analyze the reason for each question
- Prepare appropriate responses for common questions
- Compile information in a brochure

Web Sites:

Interview tips

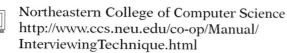 Northeastern College of Computer Science
http://www.ccs.neu.edu/co-op/Manual/
InterviewingTechnique.html

University of Maine Career Center
http://cardinal.umeais.maine.edu/~career/
int.html

Interview blunders

 Career City
http://www.careercity.com/content/
interview/during/tenbig.asp

Job Web
http://www.jobweb.com/Resources/Library/
Interviews__Resumes/9_SureFire_Ways_
to_20_01.htm

College Recruiter
http://www.collegerecruiter.com/pages/
articles/article263.htm

Common interview questions

Indiana University
http://www.indiana.edu/~libpers/interview.
html

GradView
http://www.gradview.com/careers/
questions.html

Career City
http://www.careercity.com/content/
interview/during/tenquest.asp

Keywords for Web Searches:

- interview tips
- common interview questions
- interview blunders

Suggestions:

1. This activity may be done by students working alone, but is most effective for students working in small groups. For many, the analysis and synthesis involved may be challenging; this challenge may be easier to meet in a group situation.

2. In Part I of the activity, students prepare lists of things they should and should not do in an interview. Some of the web sites they are directed to visit just describe blunders or positive approaches; the underlying rules are not stated explicitly. Students may need coaching to synthesize the information they find into general rules. If this seems to be proving a stumbling block, you might initiate a class discussion of the following (true!)

scenarios to establish the general rule: An interviewee refuses to get out of the chair until the interviewer hires him; a candidate tells the interviewer that her long-term career goal is to replace him; a candidate ignores the "No Smoking" sign in the interviewer's office and smokes several cigarettes; a candidate says he is so qualified, if he doesn't get the job, it will prove that the company's management is incompetent; a candidate announces that she hasn't yet eaten lunch, and proceeds to eat a hamburger and french fries in the interviewer's office.

3. The same problem may arise when students try to analyze the questions that interviewers are really asking. After students have compiled their lists of common interview questions, you might have the class work as a whole to analyze one or two questions to find the motivation for the question. Then have students work in small groups to analyze the rest of the questions on their lists.

4. Students should work individually to complete Part III of the activity, either in class or at home.

Selected Answers:

Part I: Do's and don'ts of a successful interview

Student answers should include most of the following:

- Research the company before the interview.
- Dress appropriately and professionally.
- Arrive on time.
- Introduce yourself in a courteous manner.
- Be aware of body language: Don't slouch, fidget, or sit in a defensive position.
- Don't speak negatively about your former employer.
- Show enthusiasm.
- Be flexible.
- Listen.
- Smile, nod, give nonverbal feedback to the interviewer.
- Ask about the next step in the process.

- Thank the interviewer.
- Write a thank-you letter to anyone you have spoken to.

Part II: Common interview questions

Student lists should include some of the following questions and sub-questions:

- Why do you want to work here? *Real question:* Are you interested enough in this position to have researched the company in advance? Are you able to make a connection between your skills and our needs?
- What did you like/dislike about your last job? *Real question:* Is your work style compatible with this company, or are you a negative person, who will tend to find fault and be difficult to work with?
- Why did you leave your last job? *Real question:* Was there trouble at your last job, which might be repeated here?
- What would you like to be doing five years from now? *Real question:* Are you ambitious, or do you just want to get a job where you can sit still for the next 30 years?
- Can you work under pressure? *Real question:* Have you developed ways to cope with stress?
- Why should I hire you? *Real question:* What can you do for us that someone else can't do?
- How do you take direction? *Real question:* Can you follow directions, or are you a prima donna?
- What is the most difficult situation you have faced? *Real question:* How do you define "difficult," and how do you handle difficulty?
- Give an example of a mistake you've made. *Real question:* Are you honest enough to admit you make mistakes? How do you deal with mistakes when you do make them—try to fix them, or hope they'll go away?

Extension:

Have students work in pairs to present mock interviews to the class, using their lists of interview questions and prepared answers.

Name _____   Date _____

Successful Interviews

Landing the perfect job requires preparation. Successful interviews result from anticipating the kinds of questions that will be asked, and having good responses. The most successful candidates know their strengths and sell those points to the interviewer.

Part I: Do's and Don'ts of a Successful Interview

Interview Tips

How do you make sure that you come across well in an interview? You start before the actual interview by finding out what interviewers expect, and what the interview really involves. A lot of resources have information on the interview process. Go to the two web sites listed below, and take notes on what interviewees should do to make a good impression in the interview.

Northeastern College of Computer Science
http://www.ccs.neu.edu/co-op/Manual/InterviewingTechnique.html

University of Maine Career Center
http://cardinal.umeais.maine.edu/~career/int.html

Now, use the information you gathered to prepare your own list of things to do for a successful job interview.

Things to Do for a Successful Job Interview

_____

_____

_____

_____

_____

_____

_____

_____

_____

_____

_____

_____

_____

_____

(continued)

Successful Interviews *(continued)*

Interview Blunders

Of course, there are things you can do in an interview that will guarantee that you **don't** get the job. Go to the web sites listed below, and look at some of the interview blunders they describe.

Career City
http://www.careercity.com/content/interview/during/tenbig.asp

Job Web
http://www.jobweb.com/Resources/Library/Interviews__Resumes/9_SureFire_Ways_to_20_01.htm

College Recruiter
http://www.collegerecruiter.com/pages/articles/article263.htm

Now use the information you found on these sites to prepare a list of things not to do in an interview. For some of the errors described on these pages, you will need to identify the underlying rule. For example, one web site describes this scenario: "When asked what motivated him, the job seeker replied, 'I've got a big house and a big car and a big credit card balance. Pay me and I'll be happy.'" The interview blunder here was focusing on the interviewee's needs, not the company's.

Things Not to Do in a Job Interview

_____

_____

_____

_____

_____

_____

_____

_____

_____

_____

_____

_____

_____

(continued)

Successful Interviews *(continued)*

Part II: Common Interview Questions

Every interview is unique. How it unfolds depends on the company, the interviewer, and the interviewee. However, all job interviews also have something in common: The interviewer is trying to see whether the interviewee is the right person for the job. Interviewers have developed questions that help them make that decision. They're not exactly "trick" questions, but the way you answer tells the interviewer a lot about you. Go to the web sites listed below, and see what kinds of questions they say are asked in interviews. Then try to decide why the interviewer might ask each question. What kind of skills can be assessed by the way you answer each question?

> Indiana University
> http://www.indiana.edu/~libpers/interview.html
>
> GradView
> http://www.gradview.com/careers/questions.html
>
> Career City
> http://www.careercity.com/content/interview/during/tenquest.asp

In the chart below, list ten common interview questions and what they're really asking. In the first column, write the question. In the second column, write what the interviewer really wants to know. For example, if the question was "Give me a specific example of something you did that helped build enthusiasm in others," the interviewer might be trying to assess your leadership skills. You could rewrite the question as, "Tell me about your leadership skills, with specific examples."

Common Interview Questions	What They're Really Asking
1.	
2.	
3.	
4.	
5.	
6.	
7.	
8.	
9.	
10.	

(continued)

Successful Interviews *(continued)*

Part III: Your Answers to Interview Questions

Now that you know what these interview questions are really asking, prepare your own answers to them. Look back at the list of questions you identified and analyzed in the last step. On the lines below, write your own answers to each question. Be sure that you answer the underlying question—what the interviewer really wants to know—as well as the question actually asked.

1. _____

2. _____

3. _____

4. _____

5. _____

6. _____

7. _____

8. _____

9. _____

10. _____

Wrapping It Up

You've found out how to prepare for an interview, what not to do, and what questions you should be ready to answer. Now's the time to share all your information with other job seekers. Put it together in the form of a brochure that tells just what to do in a job interview. Give your brochure a snappy title, and make it as easy to use as possible. Be sure to include all the main topics you've covered in this activity.

The Magic of Compound Interest

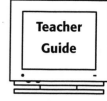

Teacher Guide

Overview:

Many people—adults as well as students—don't realize the importance of starting a savings plan early. This activity will show students how setting aside a small amount of money can add up to big savings. Students calculate a small amount that they could save every week—the cost of a daily soda. They then enter that amount in a compound interest calculator to see what that small amount would add up to over different periods of time. Finally, students use what they have learned to identify a savings goal and formulate a plan for meeting that goal.

Business Topics:

Saving, principal and interest, compound interest

Learning Objectives:

- Understand compound interest
- Formulate a savings plan to meet a financial goal

Web Sites:

 BYG Publishing compound interest calculator
http://www.bygpub.com/finance/Interest Calc.htm

 U.S. Department of Labor
http://www.dol.gov/dol/esa/public/minwage/america.htm

Keywords for Web Searches:

- compound interest calculator

Suggestions:

1. This activity should take one class session.
2. Students may work alone or in small groups to complete this activity.

3. Some students may need guidance to calculate the amount they would actually need to set aside in order to achieve the totals indicated. You may wish to demonstrate this process with a sample amount—say, $2.00, the cost of two sodas a day.

$2.00 (daily savings) × 7 (days in a week) × 52 (weeks in a year) × 50 (total number of years in the calculation) = $36,400

The total earned after 50 years by investing this sum at 10% with compound interest = $1,072,136.24

1,072,136.24 – 36,400 = 1,035,736.24.

Thus, a contribution of $36,400 earns an extra $1,035,736.24 over 50 years.

4. Once students have finished their calculations, you may wish to initiate a class discussion of the benefits of saving.

Selected Answers:

Part I

Answers will depend on the amount students enter as their contribution. Based on $1.00 for a soda and $0.75 for a candy bar, the answers would be:

1. $536,068.12
2. $18,200
3. $517,868.12
4. $938,119.21
5. $31,850
6. $906,269.21

Part II

In 2001, the federal minimum wage was $5.15 an hour. At that rate, based on the sample answers given above, the answers would be:

7. $206
8. 88.35 weeks

9. 2513.92 weeks

10. 2425.57 weeks

11. 46.65 years

Extension:

Have students work in groups to see how much they would need to save each week at vary-ing interest rates in order to have the following amounts:

$1,000,000 at age 65

$1,000,000 at age 45

Suggest interest rates of 9%, 10%, and 12%. Once all groups have completed their calcula-tions, share all results with the class.

The Magic of Compound Interest

A million dollars. How can you come up with that kind of money? Say you're 15, and you want to retire at 65 with a million dollars. Does this mean you need to save $20,000 a year for the next 50 years? No. In fact, you would probably need to save less than $1,000 a year to have a million in 50 years. How can $50,000 ($1,000 a year for 50 years) turn into $1,000,000? Two words: **compound interest**.

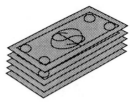

Just what does "compound interest" mean? In financial terms, *interest* can mean two things: the money a borrower has to pay a lender for the use of borrowed money, usually expressed as an annual percentage of the principal, or the return earned on an investment. In both these contexts, compound interest is interest that is not calculated only on the initial principal, but on the accumulated interest. With compound interest, you earn interest on the money you save *and* on the interest that money earns. Over time, even a small amount saved can add up to big money.

Say you invested $100, and your investment is earning 10 percent interest a year. That means that at the end of the first year, your $100 has grown by 10 percent of $100, or $10. Your principal—the amount you have invested—is now $110. The next year, the 10 percent interest is earned on the whole $110, not just the $100 you started with. So in the second year, you earn $11, not $10. Your principal is now $121. If you kept reinvesting the principal and interest every year for ten years, this is what you'd get:

Year	Beginning Principal	Interest @ 10%	Total at Year End
1	100.00	10.00	110.00
2	110.00	11.00	121.00
3	121.00	12.10	133.10
4	133.10	13.31	146.41
5	146.41	14.64	161.05
6	161.05	16.10	177.15
7	177.15	17.72	194.87
8	194.87	19.49	214.36
9	214.36	21.44	235.80
10	235.80	23.58	259.38

Without your needing to do anything, your $100 has turned into more than $250. Now imagine what would happen if you kept adding to your investment over the years—even just a little bit at a time.

(continued)

The Magic of Compound Interest (continued)

Part I: Making Your Money Work for You

Try looking at the numbers yourself. Go to the web site below, and use the compound interest calculator.

BYG Publishing compound interest calculator
http://www.bygpub.com/finance/InterestCalc.htm

For your weekly contribution, choose an amount you could reasonably save each week—say, the cost of one soda a day for seven days. Write that amount here: _____. Use 10 percent as your interest rate. Now click "calculate." Record the results here.

Year	Weekly Contribution	Interest Rate	Year-end Value
1		10%	
2		10%	
3		10%	
4		10%	
5		10%	
10		10%	
15		10%	
20		10%	
30		10%	
40		10%	
50		10%	

1. How much money could one soda a day earn for you over 50 years? _____

2. How much money would you actually have to put aside to earn that total? (Your weekly contribution multiplied by 2600) _____

3. What is the difference between the total after 50 years and the amount you would actually have to contribute (Answer 1 – Answer 2)? _____ This is the amount your money would earn for you.

(continued)

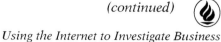

The Magic of Compound Interest *(continued)*

What if you saved enough to buy a soda and a candy bar every day? Write the cost of a soda and a candy bar here: _____. Now multiply this by seven to get a weekly contribution; write that amount here: _____. Use this new amount to calculate your savings and earnings at 10 percent interest.

Year	Weekly Contribution	Interest Rate	Year-end Value
1		10%	
2		10%	
3		10%	
4		10%	
5		10%	
10		10%	
15		10%	
20		10%	
30		10%	
40		10%	
50		10%	

4. How much money could a daily soda and candy bar earn for you over the course of 50 years? _____

5. How much money would you actually have to put aside to earn that total? _____

6. What is the difference between the total after 50 years and the amount you would actually have to contribute (Answer 4 – Answer 5)? _____ This is the amount your money would earn for you.

(continued)

The Magic of Compound Interest *(continued)*

Part II: Working for Your Money

How many years would you have to work to earn that extra money? Go to this web site, and find out what the minimum wage is in your state.

U.S. Department of Labor
http://www.dol.gov/dol/esa/public/minwage/america.htm

7. Calculate how much you would earn, at minimum wage, for a 40-hour work week. _____

8. Now calculate how many 40-hour minimum-wage weeks you would have to work to earn the amount you calculated in Question 2 (your total contribution over 50 years). _____

9. Next, calculate how many 40-hour minimum-wage weeks you would have to work to earn the amount you calculated in Question 3 (the total your money would earn for you over 50 years at 10% compound interest). _____

10. Now, subtract your answer to Question 8 from your answer to Question 9. _____ The difference is the number of weeks you would need to work to earn the same amount you could earn by investing.

11. How many years does this come to? Divide your answer to Question 10 by 52. _____ If you wanted to earn the amount your savings could earn for you, you would have to work this many extra years.

Wrapping It Up

Based on what you learned in this activity, develop a plan for saving money. Decide how long you want to save for, and how much money you want to end up with. Then use the compound interest calculator to work out how much money you will need to save every week to meet that goal.

Goal	Years of Saving	Weekly Savings Required

Comparison Shopping

Overview:

Many consumers don't have the knowledge they need to make informed buying decisions. This activity will lead students through the process of comparing different products or services.

Business Topics:

The role of consumers, decision making, research, comparison shopping

Learning Objectives:

- Understand the decision-making process
- Identify key features of a product or service
- Use the Internet to research products
- Compare different makes and models of the same product

Web Sites:

http://www.consumersearch.com

http://www.activebuyersguide.com

Keywords for Web Searches:

- product comparison
- product research

Suggestions:

1. Students can work on this activity individually or in small groups.

2. You may want to introduce this activity with a discussion of how people make purchasing decisions. Ask, How do you decide about making a small purchase—say, a CD? How would you decide about making a large purchase—say, a CD player? Do you use the same process for small and large purchases? Why or why not?

3. If students are not already familiar with the concept of the decision-making grid, you may want to work through the example, Where to Have Lunch, as a class. Make an overhead transparency of the grid on page 32, or draw a grid on the board; have students give you importance rankings for each feature and ratings for each option. Then model the process of multiplying the ranking by the rating to get a score, and totaling the scores for each option to get a total.

4. On activebuyersguide.com, the penultimate step asks for the buyer's profile. No identifying information is requested, only the following: country, zip code, gender, age range, when the purchase will be made, and whether the purchase will be made on-line or off-line. Before students complete this profile, be sure they know school—or class—policy on giving this kind of information on-line.

5. Depending on access to computers, you may want to have students print out the comparison chart they generate in Part II to study off-line.

6. *Consumer Reports* has a web site where consumers who pay a subscription fee can access product comparisons on-line. The URL is http://www.consumerreports.org. If your school or class has a subscription, have students access reports on MP3 players as part of their research.

Selected Answers:

Part I

1. Categories include memory capacity, download speed, flexibility, sound quality, appearance.

2. The site suggests other sites, noting when sites have connections to manufacturers or are otherwise biased.

Extension:

Students work in small groups to write home-page copy for a web site that helps consumers compare products. Their copy should explain to consumers why comparing products is a wise decision-making approach.

Name _____   Date _____

Comparison Shopping

You've decided to buy an MP3 player. Which of these approaches do you take to choose a model?

(A) Go to the Big Box Electronics store and buy the one the sales clerk recommends.

(B) Buy the model you saw a really great ad for in *Music Magazine*.

(C) Research the different features available, decide which features are most important to you, then check out the research to see which model with those features gets the best ratings.

Approaches (A) and (B) are certainly a lot quicker and easier than Approach (C). Unfortunately, they can also lead to your paying more than you need to, or getting an MP3 player that really doesn't meet your needs. The smart way to make this decision—or any buying decision—is to find out as much as you can about the product before you go to the store. You may still end up getting the player with the cool ad, but it won't be just because you liked the ad—it will be because it's the best player for your needs.

Part I: The Decision-Making Process

Whether you're buying a "thing," like an MP3 player, or a service, like an ISP provider, you can use the same approach to make a buying decision.

1. Identify the important features of the purchase.

2. Identify products that have the features you want.

3. Decide how important each feature is to you.

4. Rate each product according to how well its features meet your needs.

5. Compare the ratings for each choice to pick the best one for you.

Step 1. As an example, let's say you want to decide where to have lunch. First, identify the important features. In this case, important features might include cost, selection, convenience, taste, speed, setting, and socializing.

Step 2. Next, you need to identify possible choices. In choosing where to have lunch, your options might include the school cafeteria, the local pizza place, or the convenience store across the street.

(continued)

Name _____ Date _____

Comparison Shopping *(continued)*

Steps 3, 4, and 5 are easier to do if you set up a decision-making grid, like the one below. List the options as column heads. List the features you have identified as important in the first column.

Decision-Making Grid: Where to Have Lunch?							
		Cafeteria		Pizzas 'R' Us		Quick 'n' Cheap Mart	
Feature	Importance	Rating	Score	Rating	Score	Rating	Score
Cost							
Selection							
Convenience							
Taste							
Speed							
Setting							
Socializing							
Other							
Total							

Step 3. Use a scale of 1–10 to decide how important each feature is to you. Use "1" to mean "not important," and "10" to mean "very important." For example, if money is no object to you, you might give Cost a 1 for importance. On the other hand, if you really want to be able to eat with your friends, you might give Socializing a 10. Fill in the Importance column for each feature.

Step 4. Next, give each of your choices a rating for how well it delivers for each feature. Again, use a scale of 1–10, with 1 meaning "Poor" and 10 meaning "Great." Using this scale, you might rank the cafeteria as 8 for Cost and 1 for Taste. Fill in the Rating column for each choice.

Step 5. Now you need to find a way to turn these rankings into something you can compare. To do this, multiply the importance rank of each feature times the rating for each choice. For example, if you had rated Cost as 1 in importance, and you rated the cafeteria as 8 for Cost, you would multiply 1 × 8, for a score of 8. Write the score in the Score column for that choice. Do the same for each feature, and for all three choices. Finally, total the scores for each choice. Add up all the numbers in each Score column; write the total in the box at the end of the column.

Which of the three choices got the highest score? That's the one you should pick.

Of course, you'll notice that this doesn't mean that the choice you gave the highest score to is the best choice for everybody. Since the scores are based on your ranking of the importance of each feature, it's very much *your* best choice, not everyone else's. Tailoring the decision-making process to your individual wants and needs is essential. Just because one option is the best one for someone else you know doesn't mean it's also the best one for you.

(continued)

Name _____ Date _____

Comparison Shopping *(continued)*

Part II: Using the Process

So how can you use this approach to choose an MP3 player—or any other purchase? The process is just the same: identify important features, identify products that have the features you want, decide how important each feature is to you, rate each product according to how well its features meet your needs, and compare the ratings for each choice to pick the best one for you.

Sometimes, though, you don't know enough about the choices to be able to compare them this way. What if you don't know which features of a particular product are important—or you don't know what they mean? What if you don't know which products have which features? That's when you either make a purchase at random, or do some research to find out which choice is best for you.

To start researching MP3 players, go to this web site:

http://www.consumersearch.com

Find the link for MP3 players, then click on "Full Story." Read what the people at Consumer Search have to say about MP3 players in general.

1. What categories does this site use to evaluate players? _____

_____

2. How does this site suggest you do more research on MP3 players? _____

_____

3. Name three MP3 players Consumersearch reviews positively. _____

_____

_____

4. Name three MP3 players Consumersearch reviews negatively. _____

_____

_____

5. What did you learn about MP3 players in general by visiting this site? _____

_____

_____

(continued)

Name _____ Date _____

Comparison Shopping *(continued)*

Now go to the Active Buyers Guide site. This site helps consumers compare different products, feature for feature.

http://www.activebuyersguide.com

On the home page, scroll down until you see the heading "Electronics." Under this heading, click "MP3 players." On the MP3 page, click on "tips for buying MP3 players." Use this information to complete the chart below. In the first column, list some of the factors you need to consider when buying an MP3 player. Some of these factors involve choosing among several different options. In the second column, write what you would choose for each option.

Factors to Consider When Buying an MP3 Player	My Choice

Now click on the "Decision Guide" button. This guide leads you through six steps to help you choose an MP3 player: (1) Price and Features, (2) Settings, (3) Brands, (4) Tradeoffs, (5) Fine Tune, and (6) Profile. At any stage in this procedure, if you need to refresh your memory about what a specific feature or option involves, click on the name of the feature for a pop-up explanation. In Step 6, you will be asked to provide a user profile. Follow your teacher's instructions to complete this profile.

(continued)

Comparison Shopping *(continued)*

Once you have completed all the steps, you will be given a selection of MP3 players that meet the criteria you have entered. Are any of these players the same as those you listed in Part II, Question 3, as players Consumersearch recommended? If so, then make these your top choices. If not, choose three players that look interesting to you. Click on the checkbox beside the description of each player to select these three for comparison. Then click on the "Compare" button for a feature-by-feature comparison of these three players.

6. Based on this comparison, would you buy any of these players? _____

7. Write a paragraph explaining why you would or would not buy one of these MP3 players.

_____

_____

_____

_____

_____

_____

_____

8. Based on what you learned in this activity, how can consumers benefit from comparison shopping?

_____

_____

_____

_____

_____

_____

Researching Corporate Giants

Overview:

The Internet has provided a new and convenient way for business students, job seekers, and investors to get information about companies and corporations. Most corporations, particularly multinationals, have web sites that contain a lot of the information normally found in an annual report. The sites are also a valuable public relations forum in which companies can tout their business philosophies, philanthropic activities, and environmental and social awareness. These web sites provide a great opportunity for students to practice their critical reading skills.

Business Topics:

Multinational corporations; information gathering, comprehension, and interpretation; investment opportunities; career information.

Learning Objectives:

- Locate corporate information on the Internet
- Discover the history and business philosophy of major corporations
- Learn about international activities of multinational corporations
- Research job opportunities in a corporation

Web Sites:

Have each student or team choose one of the following sets of multinational corporations to research. Or come up with a similar grouping to focus on throughout the activity.

Fast-food or beverage companies

http://www.mcdonalds.com

http://www.burgerking.com

http://www.thecoca-colacompany.com

Athletic-shoe or apparel companies

http://www.nike.com

http://www.adidas.com

http://www.newbalance.com

Oil and gas companies

http://www.shell.com

http://www.texaco.com

http://www.exxon.com

http://www.bp.com

Keywords for Web Searches:

Type in the names of major corporations to reach their web sites. Using the word "corporations" or the names of products may not get you the primary sites.

Suggestions:

1. This may take quite a bit of Internet time. Be prepared. Save time by having students form small groups (2–4 students) to divide up and accomplish the tasks. You could use the activity (and the extension activities suggested below) as a simulation. Have students "set up" business consulting firms, name them, and create job descriptions for each task.

2. This activity works well with two others in this book, "Global Culture and Business" and "Global Business Ethics." However, it is not

necessary to do all three activities, or to do them in the order given. In fact, you can make the activities as simple or as complex, separately or in concert, as you wish. But completing them sequentially would give students a better overall picture of the ethos, ethics, business practices, and environmental and cultural issues of multinationals. In this activity, students locate web sites for multi-national corporations and gather information about the companies' products, history, business philosophies, international components, job opportunities, and environmental and social issues. In "Global Culture and Business," students research several countries and learn about the language, culture, and customs, devise case studies, and assemble the information into an advisory for corporate travelers and marketing departments. In "Global Business Ethics" students visit sites that monitor business ethics and multinational business activity and give more consideration to environmental and social issues such as (for example) the Bhopal, India, chemical disaster; the Exxon Valdez oil spill; "sweat shops" run by manufacturers; or the genetic engineering of foods. They also revisit corporate and cultural web sites to gather information on business practices and ethics and on social conditions in their chosen countries.

3. The web site lists are divided by type of industry. The sites named have been checked to be sure that (at this writing) they have enough information to complete the student exercises. However, with a little advance surfing, you can add to the categories or numbers of corporations for students to visit.

Evaluation:

You may use the scoring rubric at the back of this book to evaluate answers to questions and the final projects in the Wrapping It Up section (reports and ads). Extra credit might be given when students find and detail discrepancies in statements made on a company's web pages.

Extensions:

- Students may increase their understanding of career opportunities noted on web sites by visiting the Occupational Outlook Handbook on line (http://stats.bls.gov/ocohome.htm) for more details on the job title, and through checking salary estimates on sites such as http://www.salary.com.

- Have students research the history of a company's stock price and see if they can correlate its ups and downs with those of the economy, good and bad press, or environmental and social missteps.

Researching Corporate Giants

Once upon a time, when you wanted information on major corporations, you had to call or send for the company's annual report. The annual report is usually a glossy, magazine-style publication describing (in brief) the company's history, products, and recent activities. Corporations still publish annual reports for their stockholders. But a new, more dynamic public relations tool, the corporate web site, is now also available to help companies present their corporate image and promote a positive view of their philosophy and activities. The web site can be a valuable forum for corporations that have come under fire for environmental, labor-relations, or cultural missteps.

You can use corporate web sites to gather information for numerous purposes. You may want to research certain products and services. You may be job hunting, and want to see if a company's opportunities, locations, and philosophy (sometimes expressed as a "mission statement") jibe with what you're looking for. Or you may want to do research on worldwide environmental or social problems and find out how the activities of multinational corporations form part of the picture.

In this activity you will visit a group of web sites for multinational corporations and gather information in specific categories. Then you will organize and compare the information in ways that you can make use of later.

Part I: Information Gathering

Here are some groupings of web sites for multinational corporations. Choose one of these groupings to gather information on.

Fast-food or beverage companies:

> http://www.mcdonalds.com
>
> http://www.burgerking.com
>
> http://www.thecoca-colacompany.com

Athletic-shoe or apparel companies:

> http://www.nike.com
>
> http://www.adidas.com
>
> http://www.newbalance.com

(continued)

Researching Corporate Giants *(continued)*

Oil and gas companies:

> http://www.shell.com
>
> http://www.texaco.com
>
> http://www.exxon.com
>
> http://www.bp.com

Industry grouping chosen: _____

Below are some categories of information you may wish to gather from corporate web sites. This box provides enough space for one corporation. Use separate sheets of paper or your notebook for additional corporations.

Corporation Research

Company name: _____

Types of products or services: _____

Brief history: _____

_____

_____

Number of countries corporation operates in: _____

Sample countries (just name a few that interest you): _____

_____

Stated philosophy or "mission": _____

_____

_____

_____

Job opportunities of interest: _____

_____

Charitable or socially responsible activities: _____

_____

Social, labor, or environmental issues or problems noted: _____

_____

_____

(continued)

Researching Corporate Giants *(continued)*

Part II: Comparison

Compare the information that you and your group or class have gathered on different corporations. Try to summarize what you have learned by filling in each box below. How do companies in the same field compare with each other? Use the table to compare three companies that make the same kind of product.

Comparing Corporations

	Company 1	**Company 2**	**Company 3**
Name			
Recent activities/global expansion			
Philosophy/mission			
Charitable or socially responsible activities			
Acknowledged social, labor, or environmental problems			

Think About It

1. Discuss your findings with your classmates. How do companies in *different* fields compare in the same categories as above?

   _____

   _____

2. Can you make any generalizations about the way corporations present themselves on the web?

   _____

   _____

3. Did anything you learned on a corporate web site surprise you? What, and why?

   _____

   _____

(continued)

Researching Corporate Giants *(continued)*

Part III: For Further Thought and Research

1. Do you feel companies are being honest in how they present themselves? Why or why not? _____

    _____

    _____

2. Are there any foreign/global issues that interest you? What are they? _____

    _____

    _____

3. Would you like to work for one of these companies? Why or why not? _____

    _____

    _____

4. If so, what kind of job would you like to have? _____

    _____

    _____

5. What educational and career-building steps would you have to take to get that type of job? _____

    _____

    _____

6. What keywords could you use to search for more information on the aspects of multinational corporations that interest you? _____

    _____

    _____

Wrapping It Up

1. Create short reports on the companies you researched. Either do an in-depth report on one company, or compare one web-site component (such as environmental concerns or charity activities) across two or more companies.

2. Create a magazine ad for one of the companies that presents it in a positive light. You can print the company's logo from a web page to paste into your ad. Then do an ad for a social or environmental group that criticizes the company.

Global Culture and Business

Overview:

The global nature of business today makes it important to learn about cultures, manners, business operations, climates, and politics around the world. Businesspeople usually find that it is necessary to study a region of the world before trying to land the big deal. Public relations and cultural gaffes have been made when product-development and marketing departments have failed to do their research. This activity provides an opportunity for students to research individual countries from a business perspective and put the information into a format that would be useful to a company doing business abroad.

Business Topics:

International travel and trade; world geography and time zones; regional resources and cultures.

Learning Objectives:

- Research customs, etiquette, and business practices in different countries

- Explain how the influence of different cultures affects business transactions

- Outline successful tips for the international businessperson

- Begin to look at how factors such as different time zones, human and natural resources, literacy, and gender attitudes affect international trade

Web Sites:

Information on individual countries, their customs and business etiquette

CIA Factbook
http://www.odci.gov/cia/publications/factbook/index.html

United Nations' educational InfoNation database
http://www.un.org/pubs/cyberschoolbus/infonation/e_infonation.htm

International Business Ethics Forum—Thomas M. Katz Graduate School of Business, University of Pittsburgh (Use this for cultural information only; ethics are covered in another activity.)
http://www.pitt.edu/~ethics/Countries

Foreign country information for business travelers

http://businesstravel.about.com

eCountries.com/Global Business Network
http://www.eCountries.com

Web of Culture
http://www.webofculture.com/worldsmart/

Keywords for Web Searches:

- countries, nations

- business travel

- world cultures

Suggestions:

1. This activity is designed to work with two others, "Researching Corporate Giants" and "Global Business Ethics." Although it is not at all necessary to do all three activities or to do them in the order given, completing them in this way would give students a better overall picture of the ethos, ethics, business practices, and environmental and cultural issues of multinationals. Please see "Researching Corporate Giants" for a description of how they all work together. In this activity, students research several countries of the world, assemble the information into advisories for corporate travelers, and devise case

studies. This activity can also be used in concert with "Business Travel."

2. As also suggested in "Researching Corporate Giants," you can turn this activity into a simulation by having groups of students (say, four) form "corporations" or "business consulting firms" that gather the information with a specific purpose in mind.

3. Students should be able to research three or four countries in one class period if they are prepared. Go over in advance the categories of information they will be collecting, and have students choose the countries they will look at. You can print out a list of regions and countries in advance from one of the web sites. Alternatively, if you have sufficient class time, let students browse for countries that have adequate information in all the categories you wish to fill.

4. A number of these web sites include lists of hand gestures or body language specific to each country. Don't be surprised if you see students attempting to produce these gestures or if you hear them giggling. Web pages, however, usually only describe rude gestures as just that, not in detail. The specifics are left to the imagination. If you feel this is going to be a problem in your particular class, you can delete the category. Remember, though, that not all culturally unique hand gestures are rude. Some are simply nonverbal forms of everyday communication. The rude examples are usually provided only so that travelers can avoid committing them inadvertently.

5. Because we will cover business ethics specifically in the "Global Business Ethics" activity, and because the lists of web sites for that activity and this one are not identical, you might want to limit students' investigation of ethics here, even though ethics are occasionally mentioned in these web sites.

Evaluation:

Beyond completeness and accuracy, evaluate the usefulness of the information presented for the international businessperson or corporation.

Extension:

Students may select additional countries for this project to compile a class book on conducting business around the world. For example, a class of 20 students could produce a book with an impressive 100 countries if each student researched five countries.

Name _____ Date _____

Global Culture and Business

Today's global economy makes it necessary to learn about other cultures. Culture plays an important role in business negotiations and transactions. Unfortunately, many people carry cultural baggage along with their suitcases when they travel. That means they have a tendency to think their country's way of doing things is really the best. Learning about other countries and cultures in advance can give business travelers a better appreciation of different customs before their plane lands. Then they "hit the ground" ready to do business in an appropriate way.

Part I: Researching Countries

The following web sites offer a variety of information on different countries of the world. You may want to visit them each briefly (or find others) before you decide which would be most useful for the countries and topics you want to research.

CIA Factbook
http://www.odci.gov/cia/publications/factbook/index.html

United Nations' educational InfoNation database
http://www.un.org/pubs/cyberschoolbus/infonation/e_infonation.htm

International Business Ethics Forum
http://www.pitt.edu/~ethics/Countries

http://businesstravel.about.com

eCountries.com/Global Business Network
http://www.eCountries.com

Web of Culture
http://www.webofculture.com/worldsmart/

Choose two to four countries (or however many your teacher assigns you or your group) in different regions of the world. Regions may include, for example, Southeast Asia, the Americas, Western Europe, the former Soviet Union, the Middle East, North Africa, and sub-Saharan Africa. Gather information on your countries from the web sites in the categories your group or teacher has decided on.

(continued)

44   *Using the Internet to Investigate Business*

Global Culture and Business *(continued)*

Part II: Know Your Countries

You may use the chart that follows to fill in data for the first country you are researching. Use separate sheets of paper or your notebook for additional countries. As you work, try to see yourself as a business traveler who is looking for really useful information.

Country:

Cultural Features	
Languages spoken/use of English:	
Major religions:	
Different/prohibited gestures, body language (personal space, use/prohibition of parts of body):	
Manner of dress. Men:	
Manner of dress. Women:	
Sex differences in culture, society, and business:	
Significance of certain colors:	
Dining/drinking customs:	
Customs for business gatherings:	

Politics, Workforce, Economy, Other Business Issues	
Type of government:	
Population, last census:	
Percentages of population that are urban/rural:	
Literacy rate:	
Treatment of women and children:	
Treatment of workers:	
Length of workday/week:	
International time zone:	
Weather and climate:	
Major industries:	
Major imports:	
Major exports:	
State of communications and transportation systems:	

(continued)

Global Culture and Business *(continued)*

Pulling It All Together

After you have gathered all the data that you would like to, write a "business traveler's advisory" for one or more of the countries you researched. Use any charts or graphics that you need to clarify the facts you're presenting. Include information that a multinational corporation would need to conduct business in the country, especially if it intended to set up a manufacturing plant or open a retail store there.

Part III: Trade Partners

Consider any two of the countries you researched. Given their cultural differences and similarities, how do you think they would be likely to conduct trade with each other?

Names of countries: _____ and _____

1. Do they have any languages in common? Which? _____
   If not, in which language might they conduct business? _____

2. Look at their lists of major products and industries. Does each produce something that the other would like to buy? What?

   Country 1: _____
   Country 2: _____

3. Are there differences in how the countries treat workers? What are they?

   Country 1:_____
   _____

   Country 2: _____
   _____

4. Are there any customs or practices that might prevent these two countries from doing business with each other? Which, if any?

   _____
   _____

5. What time zones are they in? What is the difference in time from one country to the other?

   Country 1 time zone: _____
   Country 2 time zone: _____
   Time difference in hours: _____

   If the time difference is very great, how do you suppose these two countries would conduct business on a daily basis?_____

(continued)

Global Culture and Business *(continued)*

Part IV: Cultural Considerations in Product Design and Marketing

Some of the information that you gathered on customs, manner of dress, or leisure activities might be helpful in marketing a product or service in a foreign country. Or it might give you an idea for a product to launch. The data can also help you avoid mistakes in international marketing of products, including their packaging. For example, the color associated with death and mourning is different in various countries. Three possibilities are black, purple, and white. Yellow produces good "vibes" in some countries, and bad ones in others. Companies even sometimes have to alter the name of a product to market it in a different country, to avoid unintended associations with a similar word, or to prevent pronunciation problems.

Return to the data you collected on customs, particularly any information on use of color, shapes, the human image, and religious prohibitions. Think about introducing a product into one of the countries you researched. Then answer the following questions:

Product design and marketing

1. What product would you like to introduce in which one of your countries? _____

   _____

2. What color should it be? _____

3. What should the packaging look like? _____

   _____

4. What should the advertising look like and say? _____

   _____

Now write a short report for the board of directors of the "company" you work for on the product you would like to sell. Then design an ad to market the product in the target country.

Wrapping It Up

1. Which web sites did you find most useful and informative in this activity? _____

   _____

2. Did you come across any ideas or subjects that you would like to research further? What are they? _____

   _____

3. What keywords could you use to conduct a web search on those subjects? _____

   _____

Global Business Ethics

Overview:

Students today need a good understanding of the ethical issues facing business and industry. Ethics are not the same around the world. Perusing the web sites listed here and others will begin to give students an idea of the range of ethical standards and dilemmas.

After surveying the issues, students consider the cultural origins of business ethics. They also try to determine what the precepts for ethical marketing and business are, given all that they have learned. Ethics and business have the case study method in common. In this activity students have the opportunity to create their own case study on an issue in business ethics that interests them.

Business Topics:

Business ethics, impact of international business activities, global culture

Learning Objectives:

- Become aware of current issues in business ethics

- Examine some of the cultural origins of business ethics

- Find out about business ethics in different countries

- Use the case study method to look at a company that has behaved ethically or unethically

Web Sites:

 International Business Ethics Forum
http://www.pitt.edu/~ethics/Countries

American Quality Institute
http://www.americanquality.com

Corporate Watch
http://www.corpwatch.org

Corporate Accountability Project
http://www.corporations.org/research.html

Greenpeace
http://www.greenpeace.org

World Wildlife Federation
http://worldwildlife.org/toxics/

CIA Factbook
http://www.odci.gov/cia/publications/
factbook/index.html

United Nations' educational InfoNation database
http://www.un.org/pubs/cyberschoolbus/
infonation/e_infonation.htm

eCountries.com
http://www.eCountries.com

Business Ethics magazine's 100 Best Corporate Citizens
http://www.business-ethics.com/
100best.htm

Keywords for Web Searches:

- business ethics

- corporations

- countries

- environmental issues (and other issues on an individual basis)

Suggestions:

1. This activity is designed to work with two others in this book, "Researching Corporate Giants" and "Global Culture and Business." Although it would be most effective to have the activity here follow those two, is not at all necessary to do so. Completing them in this way would tend to give students a better overall picture of the ethos, ethics, business practices, and environmental and cultural issues of multinationals. There is an opportunity here to pull together several important aspects of business education: the role and

activities of large multinational corporations; global culture and ethics; and specific environmental, social, and economic problems affected by both.

2. In this activity, students visit sites that monitor business ethics and multinational business activity and consider environmental and social issues such as (for example) Bhopal, Exxon Valdez, and sweatshops. They may also visit or revisit corporate and cultural web sites (you may use the ones from "Researching Corporate Giants" and "Global Culture and Business") to gather information on business practices, corporate philosophies, and cultural contexts. Help students to keep from feeling overwhelmed by getting them to focus on a specific issue early on. The questions and activities throughout will provide background for the final project.

3. Teams of two would work well for the research portions of this activity. Collaborators could bounce ideas off each other, whether they're working on the same topic or not. Teams could also research and present the final project as a court case (time permitting), with one "lawyer" presenting each side. The class could be the jury, and you or a student could act as judge, disallowing certain "evidence," asking questions, and handling "objections" as needed. It would be interesting to have a student with strong analytical skills take the opposition in a case in which a corporation is generally thought to be acting ethically. What holes can he or she poke in this case?

4. It might be helpful before beginning the activity to talk about the differences between a government and a corporation. Have the class try to name five differences, and to name responsibilities that one entity has and the other hasn't. Ask for opinions: Do these entities have an equal obligation to act ethically? Why or why not?

5. As levels of difficulty go, this might be one of the more complex and demanding activities in this book. However, you may choose to simplify it by using only the first one or two of the exercises offered and exploring the topic further through class discussion.

Evaluation:

You may evaluate students on the depth of their understanding of ethical issues and on the reasonableness of their arguments for or against ethical standpoints as well as on the completeness of their assignments. A checklist for oral presentations would also help you evaluate the final project.

Extension:

Have students visit corporate web sites to see what the companies say about environmental and social issues. Examples might be oil and gas companies, footwear companies (known for hiring cheap labor overseas), fast food purveyors, paper and wood products companies. Students may choose one of the issues mentioned on a corporate web page and try to research it again using one of the sites in this activity, or a similar site. Does the chosen company's "mission statement" agree with its activities in foreign countries with regard to that environmental or social issue?

Global Business Ethics

According to the web site of the Corporate Accountability Project, of the world's 100 largest economies, about half are now global corporations, rather than countries. Let's consider that for a minute. These very large, powerful companies have the potential and the ability to get good things done. They can also, with their money and power, get around regional and international laws, take unfair advantage of workers, and pollute with abandon. They know that profits will nearly always outweigh fines. Governments, also, can become corrupt with respect to business, blocking projects unless bribes are paid. Of course there are regulations. But those are often not enough to prevent ethical breaches. Who's watching these corporations and other bodies? And how can you, as a potential corporate employee, begin to get an idea of what is right? The web sites in this activity will acquaint you with business ethics around the world, and with some of the corporations and other entities that are doing right and doing wrong.

Part I: Exploring Business Ethics

Alone or with a partner, visit some of the sites below (and others you may find) to get an idea of current issues in business ethics around the world.

International Business Ethics Forum
http://www.pitt.edu/~ethics/Countries

American Quality Institute
http://www.americanquality.com

Corporate Watch
http://www.corpwatch.org

Corporate Accountability Project
http://www.corporations.org/research.html

Greenpeace
http://www.greenpeace.org

World Wildlife Federation
http://worldwildlife.org/toxics/

(continued)

Global Business Ethics *(continued)*

As you look at the web sites, focus on issues that interest you. Here are some sample issues. You may find others.

- routine pollution/specific toxic spills

- labor relations/child labor/"sweat shops" (overworking people for low pay in poor conditions)

- financial kickbacks/bribery/lawbreaking

- intentionally inaccurate marketing and advertising

- genetic alteration of foods

- mistreatment of indigenous peoples

- exploitation of natural resources

Which issue interests you most? _____

Describe the issue briefly: _____

_____

_____

What country or countries does this issue directly concern? _____

_____

The Cultural Basis of Ethics

Individual countries can vary widely on how they view business and government ethics. Different countries may hold different beliefs about ethics, based on their religious and cultural traditions, their history, and their economy. Theory or belief may also be different from practice anywhere around the world, including the country in which you live.

Who decides what is ethically correct in a certain country? If the only way to get important things done is through bribery or smuggling, is it wrong? If your answer is yes, does it change if the product being delivered is vitally needed medication not licensed to be sold in that country, with the bribe paid by a desperate doctor? The concept this case might fall under is sometimes referred to as "situational ethics" or "standpoint theory." Something may look right or wrong, depending on where you're "standing," who you are, and what situation you're in. In some countries under some economic or political conditions, situational ethics may be the only ethics around. This doesn't, of course, mean that the people of a country agree with what multinational corporations or their governments may be doing. Corruption is a major topic for pop songs in so-called third-world countries, when musicians can get away with it.

(continued)

Name _____ Date _____

Global Business Ethics *(continued)*

Think of a situation or two that you found while viewing the web sites at the beginning of the activity. Then fill in the table.

	Situation 1:	Situation 2:
Describe the situation:		
What ethical principle seems to be displayed or violated in this situation?		
What possible cultural and political reasons could there be for this principle/ situation?		
Can you defend this principle/situation in any way? How?		
If not, on what basis would you criticize this principle/ situation?		

Researching Ethics by Country

Now go to at least two of the web sites below. Use the web sites to research the country in which the problem you chose to focus on occurs to find clues about its cultural context and the country's views on business ethics.

International Business Ethics Forum
http://www.pitt.edu/~ethics/Countries

CIA Factbook
http://www.odci.gov/cia/publications/factbook/index.html

United Nations' educational InfoNation database
http://www.un.org/pubs/cyberschoolbus/infonation/e_infonation.htm

eCountries.com
http://www.eCountries.com

Web sites I chose: 1. _____ 2. _____

(continued)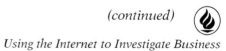

Global Business Ethics *(continued)*

After researching the country to find some cultural clues, answer these questions:

1. Who is causing the problem you're focusing on? _____

_____

2. What are some important cultural, economic, social, or political facts about the country in which the problem occurs?

Important facts: _____

_____

_____

3. Did any of these factors cause or enable the problem? Which? _____

_____

_____

4. What cultural factors would seem to be in opposition to the ethical problem?

_____

_____

5. What possible solutions would seem to be appropriate for the given country?

_____

_____

6. If you were a political leader in this country, what solution would you call for?

_____

_____

7. If you were a religious or cultural leader, what solution would you call for?

_____

_____

8. If you were a public relations consultant for the corporation or government agency causing the problem, what solution would you call for?

_____

_____

(continued)

Global Business Ethics *(continued)*

Part II: International Marketing and Ethics

Given what you've learned about global business ethics so far, how do you think marketing and advertising tie in? Try answering the following questions.

1. Do you think a marketing plan could be unethical? How? _____

   _____

   _____

2. Did you run across any examples of unethical marketing in your research? If so, describe it.

   _____

   _____

   _____

In your opinion, what ethical standards should all international marketing campaigns follow? Write your answers in the box below.

Common Characteristics of Ethical International Marketing Campaigns
1. _____
2. _____
3. _____
4. _____
5. _____

Good Corporate Citizens

Some companies are known for their good performance on ethics. These can also be found on the web. The site below should be helpful.

Business Ethics magazine's 100 Best Corporate Citizens
http://www.business-ethics.com/100best.htm

(continued)

Global Business Ethics *(continued)*

Pick a "good corporate citizen" that interests you. Then research the company through its own web site and other sources, such as news sites. Answer the following questions.

Good corporate citizen (name of company): _____

1. What makes this an ethical company? _____

   _____

   _____

   _____

2. What particular things is it noted for? _____

   _____

   _____

   _____

3. How does it accomplish its good deeds? _____

   _____

   _____

   _____

4. What does the company gain by being a good corporate citizen? _____

   _____

   _____

Wrapping It Up

Create an oral presentation on a case in which a corporation has behaved ethically or unethically. You may use the case you focused on from the beginning of this activity, or choose a new one. Use any visual aids you need to clarify your main points. If possible, use presentation software to create and augment your report. It should accurately portray all sides of the issue. Create some questions to ask your audience following your presentation. Be prepared to take questions from the audience as well.

Business Travel

Overview:

Though many businesses still rely on professional travel agencies to help make their arrangements, the Internet has also become a common tool for trip planning and making reservations. In this activity, students will use the Internet to plan a business trip. They will prepare a complete itinerary and budget for a flight, ground transportation, hotel, food, and miscellaneous expenses. Students will also look up information about weather to pack the appropriate clothing for the trip. Time permitting, students can also learn about global time zones, foreign exchange rates, and some other factors of business travel.

Business Topics:

Business travel, international travel, computation, foreign exchange rates

Learning Objectives:

- Look up travel information and compare prices on-line
- Develop a travel itinerary and a budget for a trip
- Begin to understand some other elements of travel: foreign exchange rates, weather and climate, time zones, packing appropriately

Web Sites:

Travel information, fare finders, etc.

http://www.zagat.com

http://www.fodors.com

http://www.expedia.msn.com

http://www.biztravel.com

http://www.businesstravel.about.com

http://www.travelocity.com

http://www.americawest.com

http://www.americanair.com

Weather forecasts

http://www.weather.com

http://yang.sprl.umich.edu/wxnet

http://www.intellicast.com

http://www.tvweather.com

Time zones

http://www.globalmetric.com/time

http://www.worldtimeserver.com

Foreign exchange rates

http://www.x-rates.com

http://www.oanda.com

http://www.xe.com/ucc/

http://www.businesstravel.about.com

Packing, etc.

http://www.tips4trips.com

http://www.oratory.com/travel

http://www.travelite.org

http://www.businesstravel.about.com

Keywords for Web Searches:

- travel, business travel
- airfares, flights, air travel
- hotels
- time zones
- exchange rates
- weather
- packing tips

Suggestions:

1. The business travel envisioned here does not have to be travel abroad. The activity is challenging enough using domestic destinations. However, there is nothing wrong with using a foreign business travel scenario if you feel students are up to it. That also makes it possible to do this activity in concert with at least two others: "Global Culture and Business" and "Global Business Ethics." After researching global business issues, students could "schedule" a trip to one of the countries they studied. Don't worry about being too realistic about foreign prices for meals, etc., in the budget portion of the activity.

2. Help students focus at the beginning of the activity by making sure they choose realistic destinations for their business trips. Remote tropical islands and tiny third-world countries might be difficult to find competitive fares and hotels for. Major cities and well-traveled areas will be easier to research. If students have time after completing the activity once using a major destination, you might let them do it again using a fantasy destination.

3. Expect students to ask for assistance when filling in times, dates, and destinations in on-line fare finders. Referring to each site's FAQ (frequently asked questions) or help feature should handle most common questions.

4. Make sure that any students who carry a credit or debit card do not take it out of their purse or pocket during this activity. It should be possible to search for fares without giving a credit card number and to sign off before giving any personal information. An exception are sites that demand a credit card number before searching for the lowest fare. Do not use any of these sites for the activity, although you may make students aware that they exist for real-life purchases.

5. Some budget amounts may be fictional, but all math totals should be correct.

6. Depending on the time available and the abilities of your students, you may change this to a two- or three-day business trip instead of the four-day one.

7. You may specify that students look for only coach-class seats, or if time permits, you could have them compare the cost of coach and business class. Advise that usually only highly paid or executive-level people fly business class. Occasionally, large accumulations of frequent-flyer miles allow for an upgrade to business class. Provide guidance also in what type of hotel room students are looking for. It is not necessary to stay in a five-star hotel, though if students find a very low rate on such a hotel, there's nothing wrong with using it. In business, nothing succeeds like the appearance of success! However, students should probably be looking for an average-level business hotel room.

Evaluation:

Evaluate budgets for completeness. Travel and hotel amounts in the budget must be realistic and referenced. Students will design a complete itinerary for the trip. Connection times and business activities should be realistic.

Suggested Answers:

Part III

Tips for dealing with jet lag

1. If the trip to another time zone with a difference of three or more hours is to be short, such as two or three days, try to eat and drink

at the usual home times and schedule meetings for times when you would normally be awake at home.

2. Avoid alcohol and caffeine before, during, and immediately after the flight to avoid aggravating the symptoms of jet lag. Drink a lot of water to avoid the dehydration that can also make jet lag feel worse.

3. Jet lag is usually more severe when flying east, because the day is shortened. The body, whose natural cycle is about 25 hours long, can more easily adjust to the longer day one experiences flying west. When flying east, try to sleep as much as possible on the plane and assume the day-night schedule at your destination as soon as you arrive.

Currency names

Algeria	dinar
Argentina	nuevo peso Argentino
*Austria	schilling
Japan	yen
Greece	drachma
*Netherlands	guilder
Switzerland	franc
**United Kingdom	pound sterling

*Changing to the euro (currency of the European Union) in 2002.

**May change to the euro, depending on outcome of national referendum.

Packing tips for businesspeople

Answers will vary, but might include:

1. Unless your trip is very long, or will include several different climates, try to get everything you'll need into a carry-on size bag, so that you won't be inconvenienced by the loss of checked baggage.

2. Use a roller-type bag to avoid neck and back strain.

3. Roll pants and skirts to avoid wrinkles and save room in your suitcase.

4. Lay shirts in plastic dry-cleaner bags (with hangers) on top before closing your suitcase. Plastic bags will prevent wrinkles and shirts are ready to hang up when you reach your hotel.

5. Bring only travel-size containers of toiletries. Place these and other small items in transparent, zip-closing plastic bags to avoid spillage and make them easier to find.

Extensions:

• Have students research the price of a hotel they chose on weekends for non-business travelers. Have students also research for the most reasonable rates for the same airline trip when rigid dates do not have to be held to. This will make students aware of the importance of business travelers to the hotel and airlines industry.

• After students gather information on the ups and downs of scheduling travel on-line, and travel in general, they could put together a survey of real-life business travelers. Steps might include: creating a preliminary list of concerns (the poll, gripe, or tip areas of business travel web sites might help; try http://www.businesstravel.about.com); revising and focusing the list on one specific area of business travel; creating five to 10 questions to ask; making a list of 10 to 20 business travelers to approach; conducting the survey; collating and summarizing the results; and doing a report that makes suggestions for travel services or products to address the problems voiced.

Name _____ Date _____

Business Travel

Business travel is full of questions. How far is it to where I'm going? How much does it cost? What's the weather like there? What's that in degrees Fahrenheit? What's my budget for this trip? What time do I leave? When do I get there? What time is it here? What's the time difference from my home country? If the rail schedule says the train to Brussels leaves at 20:15, what time is that on my watch? How much is taxi fare to the station? What's that in dollars? Did I get a good exchange rate, or should I go to another bank?

We can't answer all the questions above in one activity, but there are many web sites that can help you make your travel arrangements. They can help you figure out some of the many other details, too.

Pretend you work for a company with business in your country and abroad. You have to plan a four-day business trip. It is your responsibility to use the Internet to budget for a flight and hotel. It is also your responsibility to prepare the itinerary, or chronological list of where you will be at any given time. You will include meeting or convention times in your itinerary. You must assume that business will be conducted each day from 9 A.M.–12 noon and from 2 P.M.–5 P.M. local time. You will eat out three times a day. It would also be nice to plan a few leisure activities for the time each day that business meetings are not taking place.

Part I: Planning the Trip

Note a few details about your four-day trip so you can get started with your on-line airfare and hotel search. Make sure the dates of your business meetings are weekdays, not weekends. Your departure date should also be at least 14 days from today's date.

Your home base: _____

Your business destination: _____

Date and time of first scheduled business meeting: _____

Date and time of last scheduled business meeting: _____

Number of nights at your destination: _____

Remember that if your destination is far from your base, you will probably have to fly in the night before in order to be ready for business the next day! That's fine, but you must plan and budget for it. "Day 5" is included in the itinerary chart in case you have to do this.

Now use the web sites on page 60 to find a reasonable airfare and hotel accommodations for your trip. While working on-line, be sure to print out anything you think you'll need later. In fact, when making travel arrangements on-line, it is a good idea to print out or save any screens with information you don't want to lose.

(continued)

59   *Using the Internet to Investigate Business*

Business Travel *(continued)*

Travel information, fare finders, etc.:

http://www.zagat.com

http://www.fodors.com

http://www.expedia.msn.com

http://www.biztravel.com

http://www.businesstravel.about.com

http://www.travelocity.com

http://americawest.com

http://americanair.com

If you see a fare that looks good through a fare finder, check the web site of the named airline. They might offer an even better deal for the given date and time.

Flights and Hotel
Airline(s): _____
Flights (you may need to add more lines if you cannot get direct flights):
Departing from _____ airport on _____ at _____ A.M./P.M.
Arriving at _____ airport on _____ at _____ A.M./P.M.
Departing from _____ airport on _____ at _____ A.M./P.M.
Arriving at _____ airport on _____ at _____ A.M./P.M.
Airfare cost (including "departure taxes," etc.): _____
Hotel name: _____ Address: _____
Cost per night: _____ for _____ nights

The Itinerary

Now draw up your itinerary. Remember to include arrival and departure times. Also allow up to an hour each for transportation to and from the airport (depending on the size of the city), and an hour (domestic) to two hours (foreign) at the airport before your actual flight times.

(continued)

Business Travel *(continued)*

Business Trip Itinerary

Date	Day 1: _____	Day 2: _____	Day 3: _____
Time/Activity:			
Time/Activity:			
Time/Activity:			
Time/Activity:			
Time/Activity:			
Time/Activity:			
Date	Day 4: _____		Day 5: _____
Time/Activity:			
Time/Activity:			
Time/Activity:			
Time/Activity:			
Time/Activity:			
Time/Activity:			

Part II: Creating a Budget

How much can you spend on meals each day? What might you need for taxis, airport transportation, and everything else (photocopying, shoe shines, dry cleaning, breath mints, phone calls)? Below you will create a budget estimate for your trip. Estimate the cost of meals as best you can. Generally, you should budget $5–10 for breakfast, $5–20 for lunch, and $15–40 for dinner for yourself, depending on how much you eat and where. Remember, you might want to take a businessperson you're visiting out for some meals as well. If you can find any of this information on-line beforehand, so much the better. Some of the travel web sites on page 60 may help.

Travel Budget

Item	Description	Dollar Amount
Flights		
Hotel		
Meals		
Taxis, etc.		
Miscellaneous		
TOTAL:		

(continued)

Business Travel *(continued)*

Now figure the average estimated cost per day for this trip:

$_____ total budget / _____ days = $_____ per day

So, you've got an itinerary, you've got a budget. What else can you anticipate and plan for? How about weather, jet lag, and packing?

Part III: Weather, Money, and Time

Weather

How's the weather where you're going? If your trip is relatively far in the future, you might not be able to get an accurate forecast. But you can get an idea of the climate by visiting some of the web sites below.

Weather forecasts:

http://www.weather.com
http://yang.sprl.umich.edu/wxnet
http://www.intellicast.com
http://www.tvweather.com

Probable temperature range and conditions for your destination: _____

_____

Necessary items to pack: _____

_____

If you're traveling to a different part of the world and need to know generally what the weather will be like, visit web sites that discuss the climates of various countries. You can find such sites by entering search terms like "countries" and "global climate."

Time zones

Is your trip planned for a place that might be in a different time zone than the one you live in? If so, you need to find out what the time difference is and how you will deal with it.

When you make an airline reservation, the arrival time is given in local time, the time on the ground where you're going. If there is a sizeable time difference from where you live, such as three or more hours, you will have to plan for dealing with "jet lag," or your body's insistence on feeling like it would at home if you were on home time.

What time is it right now at your business destination? If you did not choose a distant city, pick one now to investigate. Use the web sites on page 63. If possible, print out a map of time zones around the world. Figure out what time zone your destination is in, what time it is there now, and the difference in hours, ahead or back, from where you are. On the day you travel, how much jet lag will you experience?

(continued)

Business Travel *(continued)*

Time zone information:

http://www.globalmetric.com/time
http://www.worldtimeserver.com

Time here, now: _____ A.M./P.M.

Time at your destination right now: _____ A.M./P.M.

Difference, in hours: _____ hours later/earlier

Local arrival time at your destination on the day you travel: _____ A.M./P.M.

Time back in your home town when you arrive at your destination: _____ A.M./P.M.

Difference, in hours: _____ hours later/earlier (Should be same as difference above)

How do you think you'll feel when you arrive at your destination? _____

_____

How might you feel six hours after that? _____

What are some ways that a businessperson might deal with jet lag?

1. _____

2. _____

3. _____

Exchange Rates

Exchange rates are used in business and economics for many different purposes. If you are traveling abroad, even though you can use a home-based credit or debit card for most things, you will still have to exchange at least a small amount of money for expenses such as carry-out lunches, taxi or tram fare, newspapers, shoe shines, etc. It is tough to budget for a foreign trip. It's not simply a matter of taking the price of an item in your home country and converting the amount to the target currency. Different factors come into play in pricing goods and services in other countries, including hidden tariffs and taxes. However, there are numerous web sites that will tell you what the current exchange rate is from one currency to another. By watching these frequently, you may be able to time a trip to coincide with a favorable exchange rate.

Foreign exchange rates:

http://www.x-rates.com
http://www.oanda.com
http://www.xe.com/ucc/
http://www.businesstravel.about.com

(continued)

Business Travel *(continued)*

Find the currencies used by each of the following countries and the exchange rate in relationship to the U.S. dollar.

Currency Converter			
Country	**Currency Name**	**Exchange Rate**	**$100 =**
Algeria			
Argentina			
Austria			
Japan			
Greece			
Netherlands			
Switzerland			
United Kingdom			

Now convert the following prices for foreign goods into U.S. dollars.

Greece: Souvenir statue @ D2700 = $_____
Netherlands: Dinner for two @ƒ 100 = $_____
United Kingdom: Cab fare @ £10.50 = $_____

Packing for the Trip

So, we've covered almost all the bases of business travel. All you need to know now is how to pack! Visit one or more of the following web sites, or others you may find, to see what information you can gather on that subject.

http://www.tips4trips.com
http://www.oratory.com/travel
http://www.travelite.org
http://www.businesstravel.about.com

Give the five best packing tips you found here. Be sure to keep business travel in mind.

Packing Tips

1. _____
2. _____
3. _____
4. _____
5. _____

News and Its Impact on Business

Overview:

A fast-paced global economy makes it essential to be aware of what's happening in one's own country and around the world. There are more sources of information than ever before. Students must learn how to find and use this information. This flexible assignment calls for students to look up news stories on the Internet that could have an impact on business, and to analyze the stories and their context.

Business Topics:

Current events awareness; information gathering, comprehension, and interpretation. May touch on: ethical and social responsibility; global culture and its effect on business.

Learning Objectives:

- Locate breaking news on the Internet that concerns or may have an impact on industry or business

- Demonstrate the ability to understand and analyze news that may affect business and the economy

- Show awareness and comprehension of the latest news events from around the world

Web Sites:

General newsgathering organizations

(most also have business news web pages)

 Cable News Network (CNN)
http://www.cnn.com

New York Times (NOTE: Readers must create a password to use this site.)
http://nytimes.com

Washington Post
http://washingtonpost.com

NOTE: You or your students can also check for on-line versions of state and local newspapers.

Just type the name of the newspaper and the name of your state and/or town into a search engine.

Current events for teens and teachers

 http://fyi.cnn.com

http://fyi.cnn.com/fyi/teachers

Business news web sites

Wall Street Journal
http://wsj.com

Forbes magazine
http://forbes.com

CNBC
http://www.cnbc.com

The Economist magazine (global news and business)
http://www.economist.co.uk

Keywords for Web Searches:

- news
- world news
- business news
- other news sources by name: *Inc.* magazine, ABC News, CBS News, NBC News, *Los Angeles Times*, etc.

Suggestions:

1. Students can work individually or in teams for this exercise. If computer access is limited, have students double up, quickly find several stories that interest them, and print out the stories (at least one general-interest domestic, one business/financial, and one international). The rest of the work can be done off-line. An exception would be the section on links to earlier stories. If you don't have sufficient computer time for the whole

class, you might demonstrate and explore this section on one computer.

2. It would be helpful to run through a news story quickly at the beginning of the activity, having the class identify the who, what, where, when, why, and how together.

3. The number of news sources on the web can be overwhelming. If you can, narrow the list of sites to those that you think would be especially relevant or accessible for your students. You might also have students seek particular kinds of stories that would touch on topics you have been discussing in class.

4. Encourage students to begin with domestic rather than international news so they can practice analyzing stories in a familiar context before stepping onto a larger stage.

5. It would be helpful to explore with students how a general interest story that might have an impact on business (a medical problem or breakthrough, a national election, a widespread power blackout) differs from a business or financial news story (a steep price increase for raw materials, a drop in the stock of a major company, the choosing of a new CEO). How does the focus widen or narrow? What guidelines or goals might the reporter be considering when writing the story? How might the audiences be different?

6. Remember to balance a business focus with a humanistic one. How might an event that is reported—or the very publication of the news story itself—affect individuals, families, the community?

7. The Internet is a very fast source of information, and it can be a good one, but it is also sometimes unreliable. Then again, newspapers and television news can also be wrong,

as we saw in the 2000 presidential election. Help make students aware of ways to verify information, whether by cross-checking with other sources, or by doing personal research. Ask: Would any business make an important decision based on one news story? Why not?

8. Students who have completed all of the activities and the extension might be interested in some of the web sites that keep an eye on the media—media watchdogs. Some of these try to be objective; some are partisan or have another axe to grind. Have students find and report on some of these sites. There may be media watchdog sites specific to the state you live in. Which, if any, of these watchdog sites are most relevant for business people?

Evaluation:

You may evaluate news summaries for completeness, and students' analysis for understanding of how events could relate or do relate to business. Extra credit may be given for analysis that considers the reliability or objectivity of the source.

Extension:

Have groups of three students form TV news teams. Two students may be news anchors who share two related, current stories with the rest of the class. The third may be a news commentator who provides analysis of the issue. After the analyst's ("pundit's") presentation, the anchors and the class may question him or her further. Then you may lead a class discussion on fact vs. opinion. What elements of the news stories may actually have been opinion, or based on biased newsgathering (intentionally or otherwise)? How close did the news analyst stay to the facts?

News and Its Impact on Business

Successful business people know it's important to keep up with the latest news. Unfortunately, many get so wrapped up in their daily routine that current events pass them by. This activity will show you how many sources of information are readily available on the Internet. You can use them to stay up-to-date on what is happening around the world. You will also learn how to critically read and evaluate an on-line news story.

Part I: The Bones of a News Story

You can analyze any news story by answering six simple questions: Who? What? Where? When? Why? and How? These questions are called the **5 Ws and an H**.

- *Who* did the action? Whom is the story about? Whom does it affect?

- *What* happened? What are the facts? What is the story about?

- *Where* did the action happen or where will it happen?

- *When* did it or will it happen? When will the next event (if any) take place?

- *Why* did it happen?

- *How* did it happen? What was the chain of events?

Basic news stories are often organized in a structure called a **reverse pyramid**. This simply means that the most important information—usually the who, what, where, and when—comes first. The story is then fleshed out with supporting details. As you read down through the story, the information becomes less and less central to understanding it, although it may be very interesting information. The key information is at the beginning of the story.

Finding and Reading the News On-line

Browse a couple of the news web sites below and find a general news story that interests you. Read the story (print it out if your time on-line is limited). Then answer the 5 Ws and an H.

General newsgathering organizations:

Cable News Network (CNN)
http://www.cnn.com

New York Times
http://nytimes.com

Washington Post
http://washingtonpost.com

(continued)

News and Its Impact on Business *(continued)*

Current events for teens and teachers:

http://fyi.cnn.com

http://fyi.cnn.com/fyi/teachers

Story 1	
Title/Subject	
Date	
Internet site	
Who	
What	
Where	
When	
Why	
How	

Now, without looking at the story again, summarize it in one or two sentences:

_____

_____

Questions

1. Do you understand the story better after analyzing it than you did when you first read it on-line? _____

2. What stands out in your mind about this story? _____

   _____

3. Does one or another of the question words (5Ws and H) seem to point out the most important fact(s) in this story? Which, and why? _____

   _____

4. Even if the story is not at all business-oriented, look at it again from a businessperson's point of view. How might this news item affect business or the economy, or what new business ideas might it suggest? _____

   _____

(continued)

News and Its Impact on Business *(continued)*

Part II: Analyzing Business News

Now read and analyze two more stories. Make at least one a business news story from one of the sites below. You can also use the general news sites listed before.

Business news web sites:

Wall Street Journal
http://wsj.com

Forbes magazine
http://forbes.com

CNBC
http://www.cnbc.com

The Economist magazine (global news and business)
http://www.economist.co.uk

Story 2	
Story title or subject	
Date	
Internet site	
Main points	
Summary	
Potential impact on business	

Story 3	
Story title or subject	
Date	
Internet site	
Main points	
Summary	
Potential impact on business	

(continued)

News and Its Impact on Business *(continued)*

Part III: The Developing Story

Web sites often provide links to earlier stories on the same subject, or to related current stories. Are there links like this for any of the stories you analyzed? If not, find a story that does provide such links. Read two to three of these linked stories.

1. What did you notice about how the story developed? Was some information reported at first later found to be false, misleading, or just incomplete? What later details increased your understanding of the story as it developed?

    _____

    _____

    _____

    _____

2. What direction do you think the story could take next? Use your reasoning or your imagination to come up with a somewhat realistic picture of what might happen next and/or how developments might affect business.

    _____

    _____

    _____

    _____

Wrapping It Up

1. Which web sites in this exercise did you find most understandable, useful, and

    enjoyable? Why? _____

    _____

2. Did you come across any concepts, topics, or ideas you would like to explore further?

    What are they?_____

    _____

3. What keywords could you use to search for more information on topics you found

    interesting? _____

    _____

Learning About Small Business and Entrepreneurship

Teacher Guide

Overview:

Most businesses in the United States are small businesses. However, more than half of new businesses fail in the first five years. At some point in their lives, many of your students will probably become small business owners. This activity introduces them to some of the many on-line resources available to help small business, often for free.

Business Topics:

Small business, entrepreneurship, franchising

Learning Objectives:

- Define the terms small business, entrepreneurship, franchise, etc.
- Define what it takes to start a new business
- Define the various legal types of small businesses
- List the characteristics of entrepreneurs
- Define the types of franchises
- Outline the pros and cons of becoming a franchisee

Web Sites:

 The Small Business Administration
http://www.sbaonline.sba.gov

Resources, forms
http://www.startupbiz.com/Doit/form.htm

Seven steps to startup
http://www.startupbiz.com/Doit/seven.htm

Structuring a business
http://www.madere.com/bizstrct.html

Small business on-line communities

http://www.ideacafe.com

http://www.biztalk.com

Entrepreneurship

http://www.entrepreneurmag.com

Franchises

http://www.betheboss.com

http://www.franchise1.com

Business plans

http://www.sba.gov/starting/indexbusplans.html

http://www.bplans.com

Keywords for Web Searches:

- small business
- entrepreneurship
- self-employment
- franchising

Suggestions:

1. This is a group of interrelated exercises that can nevertheless be used independently of each other at your convenience. The only exercise that might require some previous preparation and research is the final project.

2. Students may work individually or in pairs for most of the exercises. Students could form groups of three to design, write, and edit the brochure or booklet for the final project.

3. Since there are so very many web sites focused on small business, entrepreneurship, and franchising, it would probably be helpful for students to briefly visit a number of sites

for each exercise before settling in to collect answers.

4. Make the exercises more relevant for students by both using and asking for real-life examples of businesses in your community.

5. There is so much available on-line concerning small business, entrepreneurship, and franchising that you could teach these subjects using the Internet instead of a textbook. A good class project might be to divide your students into several small groups that would each research a different aspect of small business and entrepreneurship, print out the information they find, and assemble it as a class into a general primer on small business.

6. While we did not consider small business listservs for this activity, they represent a further opportunity for research into the problems and solutions experienced by real business owners. At your discretion, you may assign students to find and monitor one or more listservs on small business and do reports for extra credit.

Evaluation:

Evaluate on the quality and integration of information as well as the completeness of assignments. Answers to the various list exercises should be clear and concise as well as relevant to the specific subject at hand. For instance, information gathered for exercises on franchising should be specifically targeted to that, not to small business generally. The booklet or brochure final project should be evaluated for attractiveness and user-friendliness as well as content.

Selected Answers:

Part I: Getting started

Ten questions potential business owners should ask themselves

Answers will vary, but might include:

1. What do I like to do with my time?

2. What technical skills do I have?

3. Am I good at handling money?

4. What do others say I'm good at?

5. How much time do I have available to put into this?

6. Do I mind directing others?

7. What service or product will I sell?

8. What would my company's advantage be over existing firms?

9. What kind of financing will I need?

10. Am I comfortable with all of the responsibility that having my own business will entail?

General startup steps for small businesses

Answers will vary, but might include:

1. List your reasons for wanting to start a business.

2. Find the business that's right for you.

3. Research your idea.

4. Identify the market niche your business will fill.

5. Define your mission, principles, and operating structure.

6. Research and decide on a legal structure for your business.

7. If needed, find a location for your business.

8. Research and obtain any needed insurance coverage.

9. Find any needed financing for your startup.

10. Name your business, create marketing materials, and decide how you will advertise.

Ten services offered by the SBA

Answers will vary, but might include:

1. ACE-Net	Angel Capital Electronic Network. Provides options for small companies looking for investors.
2. Business-LINC	Promotes business-to-business partnering and mentorships for small businesses.
3. En Espanol	Provides information and services in Spanish.

4. On-line library	Large amounts of information available at the fingertips of small businesses.
5. Personal counseling at SBA offices nationwide	Help for specific problems and questions.
6. SBA-Net	Network of gateways to information for small business.
7. Women business-owner representatives at every district office	Long-term training, counseling, and assistance.
8. Sample business plans	Provide examples for startups to follow.
9. Disaster assistance	Loans for rebuilding at low interest rates.
10. Business loans	Financial assistance for small business. Need not be turned down by a bank in order to qualify.

Part II: Organizing a small business

Definitions of business types

Answers will vary somewhat, but those on the various web sites for this activity include:

Sole proprietorship: business owned by one individual, who receives all profits but is also personally responsible for all debts. Sole proprietorships tend to be small service and retail businesses.

General partnership: group of two or more people who run a business as co-owners. The ease and informality of organization and the legality of benefits and responsibilities are similar to those in a sole proprietorship.

Limited liability company (LLC): a hybrid organization. Consists of at least two owners who receive shares in a corporation. They have protection from personal liability as in a corporation, but get the tax benefits of a partnership. There are no limits as with the S corporation on the number and type of investors.

Corporation, C type: organization with all the essential elements of a corporation, that is, a legal entity that exists distinct from the people who invest and control in it, thus limiting their liability. Double taxation (of company profits and shareholders' dividends) applies. There are fewer limits on size and stock activities than in an S corporation.

Corporation, S type: business organization in which all income and expenses accrue to the shareholders themselves (usually a small group of owners), who then pay the necessary taxes. Liability is limited, as in a C corporation. There can be no more than 75 shareholders, all of whom must be U.S. citizens. All shareholders must consent to an election.

Why businesses should organize to limit legal liability

Answers will vary, but might include:

1. Income tax advantages
2. Reduced risk of losing personal assets as a result of a lawsuit
3. In the case of business losses, an owner may be prevented from losing more than his original investment.

Part III: Entrepreneurship

Definition of entrepreneur

Entrepreneur: person who assumes the responsibility for organizing and managing a business with the expectation of making a profit

Some common characteristics of entrepreneurs

Answers will vary, but might include:

1. Drive and initiative
2. Strong intuitive abilities
3. Curiosity
4. Ability to get along with many types of people
5. Innate talent and expertise with planning and organizing
6. Desire to be own boss
7. Ability to examine mistakes and learn from them
8. Self-confidence
9. High tolerance for risk

10. Passion for product or service that she believes she can provide better than anyone else

Part IV: Franchising

Definition of terms

Franchise: right or license to make or market a product in a particular territory

Franchisee: person who is granted a franchise

Royalty: payment made to the grantor of a franchise as a share of the gross sales or profits from that franchise

Trademark: a name or symbol that has been reserved exclusively for the use of a certain company and its franchisees

FTC: Federal Trade Commission, an agency of the U.S. government that regulates and guides business

Types of franchises and examples

The four basic types of franchises students should find are: (1) the product franchise (example: tires); (2) the manufacturing franchise (soft drinks); (3) business opportunity ventures (vending routes); and (4) the business format franchise (cleaning service).

Part V: The business plan

Parts of a business plan

The four basic parts of the business plan are: (1) description; (2) marketing plan; (3) financial management plan; and (4) management plan.

Extensions:

1. Students could look up three franchises on the Internet and compose one-page summaries about each of them.

2. Have students write a business plan for a business they have expressed an interest in starting, using the outline (shorten as necessary) found on the SBA site.

Learning About Small Business and Entrepreneurship

Large corporations may steal the headlines. But did you know that the greatest number of firms in the United States operate as sole proprietorships or other forms of small business? A small business can be anything from one person with a lawnmower to a company with dozens of employees. Potentially, anyone can start a small business. Unfortunately, more than half of all small businesses fail within five years. Often, this is because the owners did not research the business well enough before they started it, or did not take advantage of the help available to start it right and keep it going. This activity will make you aware of some of the many resources on the Internet to help small business owners.

Part I: Getting Started

Have you ever thought about starting your own small business? It might involve a product or service, or it could be an idea for a retail store or a restaurant. Handcrafting things and selling them can be a small business. So can a car repair shop, a pet-walking service, or a cleaning service.

Before you continue, think of a few ideas for small businesses that you would like to do. Keeping a small business in mind will help you focus as you look into the resources available on-line.

Business Ideas
1. _____
2. _____
3. _____

Here are some web sites to get you started. As you browse them, look for features such as questions to ask oneself, starting steps, and finding the right business for one's personality, education, and training.

The Small Business Administration
http://www.sbaonline.sba.gov

Resources, forms
http://www.startupbiz.com/Doit/form.htm

Seven steps to startup
http://www.startupbiz.com/Doit/seven.htm

Structuring a business
http://www.madere.com/bizstrct.html

Small business on-line communities
http://www.ideacafe.com
http://www.biztalk.com

(continued)

Learning About Small Business
and Entrepreneurship *(continued)*

Questions for the Potential Business Owner

Do you have what it takes to start your own business? What questions should a potential business owner ask him- or herself before signing a lease or taking out a loan? List 10 questions you found on-line below. Then, if you can, answer them.

10 Questions, 10 Answers

1. _____
_____
_____

2. _____
_____
_____

3. _____
_____
_____

4. _____
_____
_____

5. _____
_____
_____

6. _____
_____
_____

7. _____
_____
_____

8. _____
_____
_____

9. _____
_____
_____

10. _____
_____
_____

(continued)

Learning About Small Business and Entrepreneurship *(continued)*

Startup Steps

Several of the web sites on page 75 list steps to take to start your own business. On the lines below, create a basic list of startup steps for small businesses. When you can, customize these steps to the type of business you have in mind. You should have at least seven.

Steps to Startup

1. _____
2. _____
3. _____
4. _____
5. _____
6. _____
7. _____
8. _____
9. _____
10. _____

Help on the Way

The Small Business Administration (SBA) of the U.S. government maintains a site with all kinds of information for small business owners. How could the SBA help you with your small business? Search the web site http://www.sbaonline.sba.gov and make a list of 10 services offered by the SBA. Next to each service, list a specific way in which it could help a small business, perhaps one like the business you want to start.

Services Offered by the SBA	
Service	**Specific Use for Service**
1.	
2.	
3.	
4.	
5.	
6.	
7.	
8.	
9.	
10.	

(continued)

Learning About Small Business
and Entrepreneurship *(continued)*

Part II: Organizing a Small Business

There are several ways to legally organize a small business. The easiest to set up, and therefore the least expensive, is the sole proprietorship. But if you might need legal protection or some shielding from financial risk, you will want to look into some of the other forms of small business. Return to the sites named at the beginning of this activity. Use the information you find there to define these terms.

Sole proprietorship: _____

_____

_____

General partnership: _____

_____

_____

Limited Liability Company (LLC): _____

_____

_____

Corporation, C type: _____

_____

_____

Corporation, S type: _____

_____

_____

What are some specific reasons that a business would want to organize in such a way as to limit its legal liability?

1. _____

2. _____

3. _____

(continued)

Learning About Small Business
and Entrepreneurship *(continued)*

Part III: Entrepreneurship

Someone who starts or runs a small business is often called an **entrepreneur.** But a true entrepreneur is more than just someone who takes over an existing small business, buys a franchise, or works her way up through a small business to become the boss. How can you define "entrepreneur"? Visit an on-line dictionary, such as http://www.dictionary.com or http://www.iTools.com/research-it/ to find a definition. Rewrite it in your own words, given all that you've found out about small business so far.

Definition of "entrepreneur": _____

_____

A web site such as http://www.entrepreneurmag.com can help you find out more about entrepreneurs. Visit this site to fill in the information below. For the first chart, choose three entrepreneurs who interest you.

Entrepreneurs		
Name	**Business**	**How started**

Now, based on what you have read, list 10 characteristics that entrepreneurs tend to have.

Common Characteristics of Entrepreneurs
1. _____
2. _____
3. _____
4. _____
5. _____
6. _____
7. _____
8. _____
9. _____
10. _____

(continued)

Learning About Small Business
and Entrepreneurship *(continued)*

Part IV: Franchising

Franchising is a special kind of business ownership. Simply put, in a franchise, you start your own business by buying or licensing someone else's products or ideas. Franchising has definite pros and cons. The following web sites have more information about franchising.

http://www.betheboss.com
http://www.franchise1.com

Definitions

Defining the following terms should help you begin to understand the concept of franchising. Look them up in an on-line dictionary or at one of the franchise web sites above.

Franchise: _____

_____

Franchisee: _____

_____

Royalty: _____

_____

Trademark: _____

_____

FTC: _____

_____

(continued)

Learning About Small Business and Entrepreneurship *(continued)*

Types of Franchises

There are four basic types of franchises. Find explanations of the four types on a franchise web site. List them, define them, and give an example of each below.

Type 1: _____

Definition: _____

_____

Example: _____

Type 2: _____

Definition: _____

_____

Example: _____

Type 3: _____

Definition: _____

_____

Example: _____

Type 4: _____

Definition: _____

_____

Example: _____

Pros and Cons of Franchising

When you buy or lease a franchise, you take on, for better or worse, a set of rules and a structure that come with the business. Visit franchise web sites to gather a list of facts about franchising to find pros or cons. Whether a fact seems like a pro or con might depend on your personality. Topics should include at least some of the following: risks, rules, new ideas, profits, success, management, business plans, marketing plans. After you make your lists, compare them with a partner. Are there differences in how you classified facts about franchises?

(continued)

Learning About Small Business
and Entrepreneurship *(continued)*

Facts About Franchises	
Pros	**Cons**
1.	1.
2.	2.
3.	3.
4.	4.
5.	5.
6.	6.
7.	7.
8.	8.
9.	9.
10.	10.

Starting a Franchise

People don't only buy and run previously franchised ideas. They also sometimes start their own business, then sell the concept, the name, and the operating structure—again and again. This is a combination of entrepreneurship and franchising. A person who starts a franchise like this can make money through one-time fees or through royalties. A business like this can start very small and grow very large. Some examples are cleaning services, handyman services, concierge services, decorating shops, and directory publishing offices.

After cruising franchising web sites, list five ideas that you think would make great franchises.

Franchise Ideas
1.
2.
3.
4.
5.

(continued)

Learning About Small Business
and Entrepreneurship *(continued)*

Part V: The Business Plan

Before you can borrow money to start just about any kind of business, you must have a **business plan**. Investors want to see exactly how you're going to structure, manage, and market your business. Even if you don't need money to get started, writing a business plan is a very good way to focus your ideas and keep yourself on track.

The following web sites provide guidelines and sample business plans.

http://www.sba.gov/starting/indexbusplans.html
http://www.bplans.com

Parts of the Business Plan

What are the four basic parts of the business plan? Find them on one of the web sites above, and name and describe them below.

1. _____

_____

_____

2. _____

_____

_____

3. _____

_____

_____

4. _____

_____

_____

(continued)

Learning About Small Business
and Entrepreneurship *(continued)*

Your Business Plan

What business would you like to start? After looking at some sample business plans on-line, write the opening paragraph of your business plan below. Describe the business in concrete and positive terms, but don't exaggerate.

_____

_____

_____

_____

_____

_____

Wrapping It Up

Pretend you work for a small business consulting firm. You provide help and advice to people starting and expanding small businesses. Prepare an informative booklet or three-fold brochure you will hand out in your waiting room to people who come to you for help.

Here are some topics you might focus on (you may think of others). Choose one. If need be, do further research on small business web sites.

- Locating a retail business for maximum foot traffic

- What to look for in an accountant or lawyer for your business

- How to franchise your business idea

- How to market your product or invention

Insurance and Taxes for Business

Teacher Guide

Overview:

Running a business entails obligations as well as rewards. Two of those obligations are protecting one's business from unnecessary financial risk, and being sure that taxes are paid correctly and on time. But keeping up with insurance needs and tax regulations can be confusing and time-consuming. These days, a lot of help in both areas is available on-line, to be perused when the small business owner has time. Insurance companies offer on-line quotes and service. And the IRS offers information, forms, and even the opportunity to file electronically. A number of companies also sell tax preparation software. In this activity, students will investigate on-line help with taxes and insurance for small business owners. They will also look briefly at some other business-oriented web sites.

Business Topics:

Insurance, taxes, small business, information gathering, and synthesis

Learning Objectives:

- Identify the reasons for carrying small business insurance
- Practice obtaining an insurance quote on-line
- Become familiar with the tax preparation help available on-line
- Find out how to keep abreast of new tax regulations

Web Sites:

Business insurance

 http://www.zdnet.com/smallbusiness

 http://www.businessinsurance.com

http://www.insurancenoodle.com

http://www.quickquote.com

http://www.epolicy-insurance.com

http://www.travelerspc.com/commercial/

Tax information and tax products for businesses

http://www.irs.ustreas.gov/smallbiz/index.htm

http://www.irs.ustreas.gov/prod/ind_info/index.html

http://www.irs.ustreas.gov/prod/tax_regs/index.html

http://www.taxfoundation.org

http://www.taxact.com

http://www.taxcut.com

http://www.quicken.com

101 Best Business Web Sites:
http://www.winmag.com/specreps/business/101

Keywords for Web Searches:

- small business insurance
- tax preparation

Suggestions:

1. Teams of two would work well for this activity. It will make finding the information on-line easier, and will work well for the final project.

2. As an alternative to a small-business focus, you could use a consumer focus. Students could research information and quotes for personal, auto, homeowners, renters, and life insurance. They could also research tax help for individual filers and print out and complete a 1040 EZ form.

3. Insurance is not the most exciting topic in the world for most people. Real-life examples of the need for insurance from the newspaper or on-line news sources would help enlighten students. Have students who have finished the main parts of the activity find real-life examples of situations in which businesses might call on their insurance coverage.

4. Workmen's compensation laws vary from state to state. You might have students investigate why this is so.

5. You might talk a bit about buying insurance through a local business versus buying it on the Internet. What are some advantages and disadvantages of each?

6. Some quote sites may require a physical address for the business as well as other specific information in order to give a quote. To be prepared for class, it would be helpful if you went through these sites beforehand to see how far you can get with fictional information. Some sites may also require an e-mail address in order to send back the quote. If the quoting process doesn't totally work for your students, at least they can see how it is done.

7. Tax regulations can be very complex, especially for novices. For your students, who may never have prepared even an individual tax return, the information they will run across in doing the tax portion of this activity may be almost impossible for them to understand well enough to answer the questions correctly. It is more important here that students get a sense of what kinds of information are available on the web for help with taxes.

Evaluation:

Evaluate on the quality and integration of information as well as the completeness of assignments. Students should present information that is relevant to the subject at hand. For instance, information gathered on health insurance should be specifically targeted to small business, not to health insurance generally.

Selected Answers:

Part I: Insurance for small business
Definition of terms

Fleet insurance: insurance that covers vehicles owned or leased and operated by a company

Liability: legal responsibility

Umbrella policy: insurance policy that covers several different aspects of liability for a company

Health plans: insurance policies that pay part or all of an employee's expenses for medical and/or dental checkups and treatment

Property: land, buildings, equipment, and other contents owned or leased by a company

Part III: Help on the web
Best web sites for businesses

Answers may include: on-line postage buying, scheduling and tracking of shipments, on-line auctions, office-supply ordering, web site design, etc.

Extensions:

- Invite a speaker from the insurance industry to give students some real-life examples of how insurance for small business works and to answer their questions.

- Have students call local insurance agencies to see if they can match quotes obtained on-line or provide insight into why business owners might be better off with a local agency. Tell students to be sure to identify themselves as such on the phone.

Insurance and Taxes for Business

Each day of your life you face risks—at home, at school, at work. Business owners face risks, too. Someone could be hurt while driving a company car, or could hurt another driver. A customer could fall in a store or be hit by a falling tire or brick. A worker could be injured on the job. A thief could steal the day's receipts, or a vandal could break a window. Fire or flood could destroy the business site or inventory. A customer could sue for injury caused by a product he had bought. An employee might need health care for a serious illness.

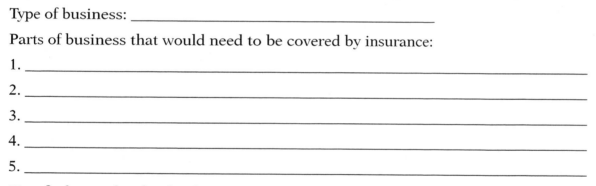

For all these reasons and more, businesses must protect themselves and their employees. For that, there is business insurance.

Part I: Insurance for Small Businesses

Exactly what kinds of insurance would a small business need? Think of a specific business, either one you would like to start, or one you know of that already exists. Ask yourself: What types of problems could cause a significant loss for the company? What kinds of events would a business have a hard time recovering from without help?

Type of business: _____

Parts of business that would need to be covered by insurance:

1. _____

2. _____

3. _____

4. _____

5. _____

Now find out what kinds of insurance are really available for those needs. Self-quizzes at the web sites below may help. Look through the web sites, then define some of the terms listed at the top of page 88.

Insurance web sites

http://www.zdnet.com/smallbusiness

http://www.businessinsurance.com

http://www.insurancenoodle.com

http://www.quickquote.com

http://www.epolicy-insurance.com

http://www.travelerspc.com/commercial/

(continued)

Insurance and Taxes for Business *(continued)*

Definitions

Write down what you find on-line about each of the following insurance terms.

Fleet insurance: _____

_____

_____

Liability: _____

_____

_____

Umbrella policy: _____

_____

_____

Health plans: _____

_____

_____

Property: _____

_____

_____

Obtaining a Quote

Now visit the sites on page 87 again and obtain a quote for one of the types of insurance "your" business needs. Before you try to get the quote, write down some information about your fictional business so you'll be ready to fill it in when it's asked for. Some sites may require more, so be ready to be inventive.

Type of insurance needed: _____

Size of physical space: _____

Number of employees: _____

Annual gross receipts: _____

Location of business: _____

Now find the quote.

Quote ($ amount per mo./yr.): _____

If you have time, get a competing quote.

Second quote: _____

(continued)

Insurance and Taxes for Business *(continued)*

Part II: Tax Preparation

Another form of self-protection for businesses is making sure their income taxes are done correctly. Filing correctly avoids fines, penalties, and interest. Preparing taxes is often overwhelming for beginning businesses, especially when they have no accountant on staff or cannot afford a freelance CPA (certified public accountant). For businesses just getting their start, or for those who do have a staff accountant to help handle things, numerous sources of information are available on the Internet to help.

Tax Information on the Web

Though tax preparation for businesses can be complicated, some owners prefer to do it themselves. Outside tax preparation can cost hundreds, even thousands of dollars. To get started, business owners may visit web sites like the following to gather information.

http://www.irs.ustreas.gov/smallbiz/index.htm
http://www.irs.ustreas.gov/prod/ind_info/index.html
http://www.irs.ustreas.gov/prod/tax_regs/index.html
http://www.taxfoundation.org

Think About It

What are the requirements for filing electronically? See what you can find out from the sites above. Put your answers in the box below.

Electronic Filing Requirements for Businesses

What are three new regulations for this tax year? Try to find them at the information web sites. Put your answers in the box below.

New Tax Laws
1. _____
2. _____
3. _____

(continued)

Insurance and Taxes for Business *(continued)*

Tax Products on the Web

In recent years, a number of software products that can help individuals and businesses have come on the market. You can learn about and order these products on the web. Tax products are like any other products to advertise. They have features and benefits. A feature is an aspect of the product, something that the product does, like compute interest or ratios for you. A benefit is what you get out of that feature, such as saving time.

Visit some of the web sites below and look at a few of the tax preparation products available for small business. Make a list of some of the features of a product that the advertiser emphasizes. Then find out or figure out what the benefit of each feature would be.

http://www.taxact.com
http://www.taxcut.com
http://www.quicken.com

Tax Software Products and Features		
	Feature	**Benefit**
Tax Product 1: _____		
Tax Product 2: _____		

(continued)

Insurance and Taxes for Business *(continued)*

Part III: Other Small Business Help on the Web

The World Wide Web has added another dimension to starting a small business. Information, advice, and communities of like-minded business people are all at your fingertips. Numerous services are also springing up on the web to enable sole proprietors and other small businesses to act like big businesses and have some of their advantages. A web site like the one below rounds up many of these services.

> 101 Best Business Web Sites
> http://www.winmag.com/specreps/business/101

Make a list of some of the other kinds of help for small businesses available on-line.

On-line Help for Business

1. _____
2. _____
3. _____
4. _____
5. _____
6. _____
7. _____
8. _____
9. _____
10. _____

In your opinion, what are three of the best things available on-line to help small businesses, and why?

1. _____
   _____
2. _____
   _____
3. _____
   _____

Wrapping It Up

With a partner, role-play a scenario that will show why small business owners should have a certain type of insurance. First write out the pros and cons of the insurance product. Then find the costs, and the list of items covered. Have one person play a business insurance salesperson, and the other a reluctant business owner. Write your scenario in script form and perform it for the class.

Appendix

Business Education Web Sites

The National Business Education Association
http://www.nbea.org

Marketing Education Association
www.nationalMEA.org

Association for Career and Technical Education
(Business Education Division)
www.acte@acteonline.org

Business Professionals of America
www.bpa.org

DECA (an association of marketing students)
www.deca.org

Future Business Leaders of America—
Phi Beta Lambda
www.fbla-pbl.org

JumpStart Coalition
www.jumpstartcoalition.org

National Council on Economic Education
www.nationalcouncil.org

Southern Business Education Association (SBEA)
www.westga.edu/~sbea/

Mountain-Plains Business Education Association
(M-PBEA)
www.fhsu.edu/mpbea

Western Business and Information Technology
Educators (WBITE)
www.wbite.org

General Scoring Rubric

The general scoring rubric below shows some of the factors that might be considered when scoring students' work.

4 Exemplary Response
Student's response clearly shows an in-depth and thorough understanding of the activity's business concepts and content. Written assignments are clear, concise, and insightful. Computer presentations are interesting and easy to follow. Overall, the response exceeds expectations.

3 Competent Response
Student's response shows a good understanding of the activity's business concepts and content. Written assignments are reasonably clear and thoughtful. Overall the response is solid with a few minor discrepancies.

2 Satisfactory Response
Student's response shows some understanding of the activity's business concepts and content. Written assignments are attempted but may be incomplete or unclear. The assignment contains errors and overall, the response is below expectations.

1 Unsatisfactory Response
Student's response shows little or no understanding of the activity's business concepts and content. Written assignments are incoherent and the assignment contains numerous errors. Overall, the response is unacceptable.

0 No Attempt
Student makes no attempt.

We want to hear from you! Your valuable comments and suggestions will help us meet your current and future classroom needs.

Your name_____Date_____

School name_____Phone_____

School address_____

Grade level taught_____Subject area(s) taught_____Average class size_____

Where did you purchase this publication?_____

Was your salesperson knowledgeable about this product?   Yes_____   No_____

What monies were used to purchase this product?

___School supplemental budget   ___Federal/state funding   ___Personal

Please "grade" this Walch publication according to the following criteria:

Quality of service you received when purchasing .... A   B   C   D   F
Ease of use... A   B   C   D   F
Quality of content.. A   B   C   D   F
Page layout .... A   B   C   D   F
Organization of material .... A   B   C   D   F
Suitability for grade level .... A   B   C   D   F
Instructional value... A   B   C   D   F

COMMENTS:_____

_____

What specific supplemental materials would help you meet your current—or future—instructional needs?

_____

Have you used other Walch publications? If so, which ones?_____

May we use your comments in upcoming communications?   ___Yes   ___No

Please **FAX** this completed form to **207-772-3105**, or mail it to:

Product Development, J. Weston Walch, Publisher, P.O. Box 658, Portland, ME 04104-0658

We will send you a **FREE GIFT** as our way of thanking you for your feedback. **THANK YOU!**